LIGHT
AT THE END OF THE
BOTTLE

LIGHT
AT THE END OF THE
BOTTLE

Judged by All, Helped by Few

VANESSA BIRD

Contents

INTRODUCTION

Everyone has their own opinion of alcoholics. I've heard it all - *complete wasters; selfish idiots; well, I can drink normally; it's just about having willpower; if they just find the trigger, they can cure it*...the list goes on. In this day and age, we accept obesity and anorexia and many other mental disorders as forms of mental illness. Some are issues that could be classed as self-inflicted, or a choice, which is no different to alcoholism. Although from my personal experience I can tell you it certainly didn't feel like I was choosing to be an alcoholic, there didn't seem to be a way out of it once it spiralled out of control. These illnesses often lead to physical problems not to mention the emotional torment so why should alcoholism be any different? However, alcoholism remains a dirty subject to what seems like the majority of people. There is help available however I question some of the workers in these fields as to whether they actually understand it. Do people really choose to just drink their life away? Can they just stop if they wanted to? It is because they are just weak? These are the questions and assumptions made by people who do not know what it is like to suffer with alcoholism or addiction.

People assume it is because the person is weak but the people who suffer usually have very strong traits. The general assumption seems to be that addiction is a choice whereas people who have suffered know this just isn't the case. I experienced so much judgement from all, including the health profession, as to why I was doing it to myself. There wasn't a clean-cut answer and I'd got so dependent on alcohol that I couldn't see any way out. I didn't feel like I'd 'done it to myself' but that it was happening *to* me. Why isn't it properly classed as a mental illness, after all, what I went through was totally mental? There are many questions and very few answers, other than from the opinionated and holier-than-thou types or people who think they know about the subject but have no direct experience of it themselves. We don't even know about the amount of people that isolate themselves while in active addiction and barely leave their homes other than to get their next fix. However, as a society we prefer to turn our back on these issues and pretend they don't exist, or exist only for the losers. Alcoholics are told to stop drinking like this is new news to them, it isn't at all helpful. The help I personally needed was around staying clean long-term. I could get myself off for a time but always ended up drinking again later down the line. I was signed off from an alcohol and addiction centre for being sober for a week which didn't help me at all. This was dangerous for me, believing I was 'cured' which lead me back to thinking I could be a 'normal drinker'. I was physically addicted and didn't know how to live without alcohol, even though I clearly couldn't live with it. All alcoholics and addicts try to go it alone initially as it's a very touchy subject. It breeds self-loathing and low self-esteem, and most are too embarrassed to speak up or too confused as to whom to turn to in their darkest moments. Also, not many people have the privilege to be able to pay to go into rehab. When it feels like the majority of the population are so opinionated on this subject, it makes the sufferers feel even more vulnerable trying to approach others for help. If there were more understanding and help with abstinence-based recovery, people who are struggling would have the help to turn their lives around and lead a healthy lifestyle. If people could turn their life around, before drinking or drugs consumed them, in my opinion, it could free up some much-needed bed space in hospitals and help relieve the overcrowding in prisons. Alcohol and drug use doesn't just destroy the person using, it also affects all who are close to them. If there were more awareness and help it would lead to far more than just the addicts receiving help. In this day and age, people are becoming more open-minded and yet this remains a taboo subject. Either people want to voice their judgemental opinions, or they just turn away as it isn't their problem. Alcoholism can happen to anyone. Are people born with addiction? Is it just something that happens to them? Is it something in the brain that causes it? My aim is not to explore the scientific reasoning. My aim is to bring some awareness of the subject and to tell my story. My story of what it was actually like in the depths of despair during active alcoholism. This is only my opinion and in no way am I trying to preach or state what is right or wrong or contradict any current help that is available. It is still very important to seek medical advice if you have an issue. I don't believe there is a right or wrong approach when it comes to addiction, however I believe abstinence-based recovery is the only way forward, in whatever channel of support someone chooses. Usually, addicts can come off their substance for a time - some a few days, some a few years - but the problem is remaining off it. It's the thinking that controls the drinking. I heard, whilst in recovery, that when an alcoholic or addict stops drinking or using, they go back to the emotional age of when they first picked up. I'm not sure if this is a proven fact, but I was in my early thirties when I had my last drink but emotionally, socially, and behaviourally I felt like a teenager, so I believe there is some truth in this statement. I wasn't sure how to behave and literally had to start learning how to feel again.

This is purely my experience and I am writing this to bring more awareness and to speak openly on the subject and how it has affected my own life. If I can help just one person through the despair in letting them know that there is light at the end of the tunnel, then I've achieved what I set out to do. I cringed as I wrote some of this, but I believe I needed to be totally honest in what happened so that others can also grow stronger in being honest with themselves.

Although I personally didn't have great success when I sought help through 'the system' I want to emphasise again, that if you do have any problem with alcohol or drug use always seek medical advice first. The UK has some of the best medical professionals in the world and do a fantastic job in our society. Always get yourself checked over physically by your local GP or medical professional. I wholeheartedly support abstinence-based recovery, but it is so important that you get your physical health checked first so you can then work on your mental health.

EARLY LIFE

I start with my early life as whenever I sought help with alcoholism I was always asked about my childhood. The general view seemed to be that something must have happened to me at some point in my life which turned me to alcohol, so I was always asked to start from the beginning. This is a brief summary of my early years, in the attempt to show that alcoholism is a progressive illness. Some people may have emotional issues they try to sooth with drink or drugs but for others, and me, drinking steadily spiralled out of control and into alcoholism. Before I knew it, I was a full-blown non-functioning alcoholic and I had no idea why.

I was born in May 1980. Growing up I lived with my mum, Paula, my dad, John, and then baby David came along when I was two and a half years old. It's a cliché but I really had a happy childhood.

My earliest memory, however, wasn't great. Baby David was born, and no one came home. I felt abandoned and my Nanna came to stay to look after me. I was excited about David coming home and looked forward to having a brother to play with. Mum went into hospital to have him and then it was just me and Nanna for a while. It probably wasn't very long at all, but I was very young, confused, scared and didn't know what was happening. One moment things were fine then there was no Mummy and Daddy and no sign of baby David. I remember clinging to Nanna, absolutely fretting. I made myself ill with worry and vividly remember throwing up all over the bed and her holding me. This seemed to be a trend in later life, throwing up in bed, but I was only little and had worked myself into a right state. Daddy would come home from work briefly then be straight out again to the hospital and I was probably asleep by the time he got home. My brother was born with no soft spot on his head so his brain wouldn't have been able to grow properly. My mum kept telling the doctors there was something wrong with his head, but they just told her to stop worrying and that she was just being an over-concerned mother. However, they did end up finding something. David had to go to Great Ormond Street and have his head drilled open to have surgery at only a few weeks old. Obviously, at my young age I wouldn't have understood any of this. I just felt abandoned and very, very scared. Luckily the surgery went well and everyone eventually came back home.

When growing up David and I played well together and there were no barriers in our games, he would play along with my Barbies with me while I would get involved with his wrestlers and cars. We would make up games to keep ourselves amused, I never remember feeling bored. We made up games like Tree to Tree, one of us had to get from one tree to the other in our garden without the other catching us. Or Knees and Bum, we had to try to get the other's knees or bum onto the floor to win, this one usually involved a few bruises. My nickname for David is Div and I've called him that ever since we were kids so that's how I will refer to him. It's not because he acts a div (well, he does at times) it stems from some Irish friends of ours when growing up. They pronounced David 'Divad' so that's where it started and over the years, I just shortened it. We were happy children. We used to particularly look forward to our holidays at our Nanna's in Hastings. She lived in a bungalow and had a huge garden that we would play out for hours in. My dad used to chase me around the garden squirting water at me from an old washing up liquid bottle and I would run around in my swimsuit screaming with laughter. It always seemed to be brilliant sunshine when we stayed at Nanna's. Whether that was just due to the time of year I have no idea, but we were always getting splodged up (Dad's word for sun cream) and going to the seafront, playing crazy golf, eating huge chocolate chip cookies from the stalls and going to look at all the fish in the tanks at the De La Warr pavilion. If we weren't staying at Nanna's we'd holiday at holiday parks which I became totally addicted to the excitement of.

I was quite a shy child and all my school reports stated, 'Must speak up more in class'. It didn't matter that I was able to answer the questions or write them down, apparently, you are a bit stupid unless you are willing to be Billy-big-mouth and announce it to everyone. I never felt very comfortable with this and remember Mum having conversations at the school on numerous occasions stating that I was just shy. Being shy I used to love holiday camps as I could sit and watch, secretly observing what was going on. I adored everything about the holidays, the music, the glitter ball, the party dances, the shows, and the entertainments team used to amaze me. I couldn't comprehend how they could have that amount of confidence on the stage and with talking to people. I used to look at them in awe and wish I could be like that. When I grew up my ambition was to be a blue coat. The only problem was if someone so much as asked me my name I'd cower and hide behind Mum. Apparently, I didn't have this issue as a very small child. I used to sit on the end of the pram that Div was in (Mum had one of those huge things that took up the whole pavement and could fit about twenty-six kids in), and if she stopped to talk to someone I'd give them a filthy look, smack my arm down and shout, "No talk to that lady". A right charmer I was before the shyness kicked in. Just as well it did, I suppose.

Christmas was another time of year I loved when growing up, who doesn't? We'd stay up late and somehow Div would hear the sleigh bells in the night and we'd wake up extra early to our stockings. Div and I would rush into Mum and Dad's bedroom in the early hours to get them up. Nanna would always be there too for Christmas, so she wasn't excused of the early wake ups either. We used to get a big sack each full of presents and be so excited all day. After Christmas dinner, Mum and Dad would be dozing in front of the telly, shattered after the extra early wake up and looking after over-excited kids. Nanna would be doing that nodding thing old people do and say she hadn't been asleep, even though we'd heard the snoring, so Div and I used to keep the noise down and play nicely. We'd sit and put Lego together and show each other all our presents and just be content and happy.

On Boxing Day Nanna, my mum's mum, used to go back home to Hastings then Grandad, my dad's dad, used to turn up. Grandad was such a cool Grandad and from the moment he arrived, if he wasn't nodding in his armchair with some Western blaring out, he'd be sat at the dining room table and we'd play board games or cards the whole time. He used to come to stay once every three weeks. All in all, everything was happy in our household. We never got bored. Mum used to have to work at weekends, so Dad used to take us over the park to find squirrels, feed the ducks, collect conkers or jump in puddles.

So, for someone growing up so happy and full of life what happened? How did I end up a non-functioning alcoholic? How did I lose nearly everything, including my life?

TEENAGER

At school I was still quite shy, but I had a wide group of friends. I was friends with the 'in' crowd but also friends with the 'not so in' crowd so I had no issues although my memories of secondary school weren't the best. Nothing happened or went wrong I just didn't feel very comfortable. I was constantly worried about being picked on in front of a class full of kids. Although I could play up at times and hold my own with the teachers, I just didn't feel like I fitted in. This was a trend in later life, always feeling like the outsider and almost feeling lonely even in a room full of people. I can't really put my finger on it even now, but I just didn't feel right at school, the shyness being the main factor I believe. I used to dread drama lessons. I absolutely hated them and if there was any lesson I would try to bunk off from it was that one, although everyone else loved it.

When I got to fourteen or fifteen I'd be out with my mates. I had some really close friends. In our year group everyone got on well and we tended to go out mob-handed. I guess we were kind of intimidating to other people as there would literally be about seventy kids gathered together on the Green and we'd have the police turn up a lot. We'd never really done anything bad, we just used to meet up and drink Thunderbirds, 20-20, White Lightning or K cider. One of us would wait on the street corner for someone passing to go in the offy and we'd ask them to get us some drink. If we persisted long enough someone would oblige. We used to have to change drinks quite often as the people in the offy got wise as to why so many people were buying bottles of Thunderbird. We used to neck a bottle, spin around a few times then sprint up a hill and back to really get the alcohol kicking in. Looking back, we were dicks, but this is just part of growing up and I guess most kids go through it when they experiment with drinking. From the first moment I tried it, I fell in love with alcohol. To me it was confidence in a bottle, and I could be who I wanted to be and not have to hide away, trapped by shyness. I don't remember my actual first drink, but it was always about when we were growing up. There were often stumpy bottles of beer in our house as Mum and Dad used to like a few in the evening to unwind. We'd sometimes stop at pubs on the way to Nanna's or at weekends for a lemonade and a packet of crisps. Don't read into this, Mum and Dad didn't have an issue with alcohol, they just drunk a few beers every now and then. However, when I discovered it, it opened a whole new life to me. During those evenings out with mates over the park, I'd always seem to have to overdo it more than anyone else. I'd always have to be that bit bolder and go that extra bit more but that's me all over, all or nothing.

As I already mentioned, when growing up we used to stay at holiday parks. When I was fifteen, we stayed at a place called the Savoy Holiday Village in Yarmouth, Isle of Wight. It sounds much posher than it was, this place was literally stuck in the seventies down to the curtains, carpet and furniture. It seemed to be stuck in a time warp. However, it had a magical pull to it. Being quite a small park, everyone got to know the staff and other holidaymakers and it lived up to its name (not the Savoy part), it was like a little village. I'd watch Mum and Dad play bingo and want to be the bluecoat calling the numbers and would sit and observe. I will call one of the bluecoats Dean. Dean couldn't sing or dance and was overweight, but he was an excellent compère and used to run the kids club. All you would hear is little kids shouting out, "Uncle Dean". I don't know what it was about him. Actually, yes, I do. It was the fact that he was on stage and all eyes were on him that I fell for him, and fall for him I did. When we were leaving and handing in the keys at the end of the break, we decided we'd go back the following year. Mum and Dad always liked trying new places, so we never went back somewhere we'd already been. This time it was unanimous, we just had to go back.

The following year we visited the Savoy again (it sounds so grand when I put it like that). I was allowed to take a friend along and I spent my sixteenth birthday there. I'd told my friend how there was a bluecoat called Dean that I fancied and was nervous to see him again. Bear in mind at this point he had no idea who I was, I just used to sit and watch and had never so much as spoken to him. As expected, he was there in reception doing the meet and greets. My knees turned to jelly, I just loved him. I knew it was love. It could have been an obsession, I kind of was obsessed, but whatever it was I was besotted. Had I have met him anywhere else, at school or on a bus, I'm sure there would have been no attraction, but in the holiday camp environment he was the man and everyone knew him, and I just loved him.

We had the time of our lives and now we were older we were staying up after Mum and Dad had gone to bed. We made friends with other teenagers and would all sit in the ballroom together after the entertainment had finished. One night Dean was there. I felt sick with lovesickness. The nerves were there, I was buzzing, and the butterflies were hammering away in my stomach. He sat at our table. I thought wow, how amazing, Dean was sitting opposite me. I told myself to look cool, look like I'd got it together. So, I challenged him to an arm wrestle. This was probably the most uncool thing I could've done at the time. He was twenty-four, I was sixteen. What to do? - arm wrestle obviously. Also, I have always been slight, so I was probably about eight stone and he was probably about sixteen stone, but of course the thing to do was challenge him to an arm wrestle. He accepted. OMG, he actually accepted. I was drunk, love drunk, drunk-drunk, off my head with ditsyness and alcohol. We arm wrestled, he won, and I 'accidentally' fell onto him. Wow, what a smooth mover I was. We ended up kissing. All that was going through my head was *I'm snogging Dean*. The same Dean who was on the stage. The Dean who I'd thought about for the past year. The Dean who everyone at the holiday village knew like he was famous.

The next day I saw him when I was with my parents. I tried to look like I was together. I really didn't look together. I probably tried to say something, but it came out in Japanese or some other language that even I didn't understand, so it turned into a little giggle and this mess of noise just escaped my mouth. Luckily Dean was older and a bit more with it so he just went on in his happy-go-lucky way and talked to Mum and Dad. Div had earned the nickname Sonic, so given by Dean himself. At some point, Div had been swimming and left his clothes in a bag around the outdoor swimming pool. A breeze had got up and blown his clothes about, including his Sonic the Hedgehog pants. He was known as Sonic for the rest of the break much to his embarrassment.

The following year we returned on our Whitsun break. I was with another friend this year, Christine, who was my bestie at the time. We each had a pint on the ferry crossing which was really classy for two seventeen-year-olds. We were cool, what can I say? That pint on the ferry was my pint of confidence. The same happened, we met up with old friends I'd met the previous year and it was like one big family. We drank, we stayed up late, Christine pulled another bluecoat and I was obsessing over Dean and we were back together. I never heard from Dean when I left the holidays. I might've got the odd phone call, literally out of the blue, that took my breath away. We asked how each other were then ran out of conversation so they were really awkward phone calls. He always called about a week before we were due to go there on holiday to make sure I will be there and to ask if, "Things will still be the same with us". What a mug I was but it didn't matter to me at the time.

At sixteen I didn't know what I wanted to do when I left school. I got reasonable GSCE results which was surprising considering I'd literally done no revision. The revision break should have been that week we had off at the end of May, but I had been at Savoy and had 'forgotten' to take my revision with me. I was caught in the predicament of what to do. As I didn't know what I wanted to do I stayed on to do my A levels which was odd as I didn't particularly like school. If I remember correctly, I completed a year, then during the first week back after the summer holidays, I decided in the middle of a double Psychology lesson that I couldn't do it anymore. I went around to all my teachers to let them know I was leaving. It was one of those rare occasions where I decided on the spot and just knew deep down it was the right thing to do, then saw it through. It was scary but also very liberating and I felt like a great weight had been lifted from my shoulders. My mum used to work at the school and all the teachers knew her so I had the usual, "What would your mother think?" conversations. I was used to those sorts of comments but obviously no one else used to get that treatment. I remember thinking my parents would be mad at me, but the opposite happened. They were absolutely fine and were more pleased that I'd made up my mind to do something, they knew I only went back as I didn't know what else to do with my life. During the six weeks holiday the previous year my dad had got me some summer work in an office for a bank. He worked there and got me a work placement in a different office. I was put in the systems liaison department which basically did all the IT jobs the IT department didn't want to do. I liked the people and I liked the work. It helped that I'd also done a secretarial course at the same time as my A levels and was able to create any forms they needed. Just before I left the six weeks they asked if I wanted to stay but I'd stupidly said no as I was going back to do my A levels. I made a call back there and spoke to one of the managers. They got me in for an informal interview and I had my first proper job. I couldn't have been happier. My life literally changed overnight, and I have no regrets at all about leaving school, I was just shocked I had it in me to do it.

By this time nearly all my mates had been on holiday to the Savoy with me as we were now going about three times a year. I'll never forget a call I received from my friend, Leanne. She was bursting with excitement and called to tell me that she'd got a job...at Savoy. My Savoy. With my Dean. On my Isle of Wight. I really was chuffed for her, but I was also so envious. How did she have the bottle to do that? She managed to get a job as a waitress there. I had been at the bank for a year or so at that point and she asked if I wanted to go with her. I didn't know what to do. Live and work at a holiday camp, the place I adored being at, or stay at home with my now long-term(ish) boyfriend and my grown-up job? I was mainly gutted because I didn't have the courage to up and go as she had. She was so happy. I really was happy for her, but I just didn't feel like I could do it. My head ruled my heart on this occasion, and I stayed put.

I was doing well at Barclays. I worked my way up to team leader (only of a team of three, me being one of them) and I was still really enjoying it. The department had split and I was on the helpdesk, taking calls for computer issues then going out around the building to fix them. I've never had any idea about IT and am not an IT geek at all, but I got on well. If someone showed me what to do they only needed to do it once and off I went and got the job done. The bank offices were like a big family. Both my mum and dad had worked there which was how they met. Everyone knew everyone and there were a lot of kids of parents who worked there, me being one of them. From work, I gained confidence in the three years I was there. I was very ambitious back then and there wasn't really any progression from me where I was. My boss left and I was never going to get a manager's job at the age of twenty and there wasn't an opening in second line support which was the natural progression, so I decided to look elsewhere. At this point, I was seeing someone else, a new long-term(ish) boyfriend. I moved into his house in Surrey, so it made sense for me to look for work in that area. I secured a first- and second-line IT support job in Epsom and again got on well there. Being in IT, I was used to working mainly with men. When I was younger and throughout school, I had a lot of boy-friends. I put in a hyphen because I mean friends, not boyfriends. I just seemed to get on better with men than women.

VISIT TO THE ISLE OF WIGHT

During my time working in Epsom, my friend Claire and I decided it was time to go back to the Isle of Wight and visit Leanne. We hadn't been to the Savoy for a while and hadn't been since Leanne started working there. I was nervous as although Dean wasn't working there anymore, I knew the chances were I'd bump into him, I'd heard from Leanne that he often popped in to say hello to some of the guests he had known over the years. Leanne had got a job on the entertainments team so was now a bluecoat. I was really pleased and excited for her. I wasn't even jealous although she had my childhood dream job, I would never have had the bottle to have done it. Claire and I sat in the audience like proud parents watching her do the show. When the show had finished, we went to the bar and ordered two large vodka and cokes with ice. I know it had ice in even after all these years as when I turned around with a glass in each hand, I came face to face with Dean. My world seemed to freeze there and then. Everything seemed to go silent other than the clanging of the ice in the glasses due to me shaking so much. I believe I just stood there with my mouth open. I still hadn't mastered being cool. After what seemed like an eternity of silence, he said four words, "We need to talk". I think I just nodded. I probably necked the vodka and got a few more in before I went for that talk. We sat outside in a fresh starry night on a bench outside my chalet. He quite simply said, "I want to marry you". My life turned upside-down in an instant. The drive home after that break was awful. I think I practically had a meltdown whilst waiting for the ferry. I was bawling my eyes out with snot-bubbles, going over and over to poor Claire about what I was to do. I had no idea. My life at home was quite simple. OK, I was living with someone who I didn't really like, let alone love, but I think I'd managed to convince myself I loved him. I was pretty sure the feeling was mutual. I had a job I really enjoyed and was earning decent money. Then Dean showed up in my life again and my head was spinning. I was suffering from exhaustion, no doubt a hangover, confusion, and really thought I was breaking down. Claire offered advice and was there for me, but it couldn't have been a very nice journey back for her. I arrived back at home and I don't think I said much to my boyfriend other than, "I'm tired", and went straight to bed.

I had made my mind up. I handed in my notice at work and was going to move to the Isle of Wight. To Dean. To the teenage love of my life. This coincided with another thing that happened that had a huge impact on my life.

DAD

I was back at home and it was November. My trip to the Isle of Wight had been the month before. I'd had a messy breakup with my ex which had turned nasty. I was trying to get my head around moving and I was working my notice. I had no job to go to. Everything was up in the air and change was all about me.

Dad used to suffer from indigestion and sometimes after he'd eaten, he'd announced he'd, "Done his trick", and he'd suffer for an hour or so in pain. I believe he was on some sort of gardening leave from work before he retired, life at this time was a bit of a blur so I'm not really sure what was going on. I was steadily drinking. Not enough to call it a problem, but enough. By this age, hangovers had started to kick in. When I was younger, I didn't know what one was, but as the years rolled on, they were getting worse and worse. I was twenty-one. My dad went to bed with indigestion. I was sleeping on the floor as I'd moved out so no longer had a room, when we were woken by an awful gurgling noise. My mum rushed about screaming, "John". The noise was coming from my dad. Everything stood still. Everything moved so fast. Mum was on the phone, calling for an ambulance. Div was dazed and confused and on crutches. He had broken his tibia and fibula the year before in a football accident and had just had the metal pins removed from his leg. He was pumped full of medication and in shock so just stood in the doorway. Mum was shouting down the phone. The ambulance wasn't there yet, and Dad wasn't breathing. The horrible noise came to an abrupt stop. I grabbed the phone and started screaming for the ambulance. Where was it? We were only just over a mile away from the nearest hospital. The lady on the call started talking us through mouth-to-mouth. Mum tried, nothing. I took over, nothing. I continued. Mum continued. We took turns counting. This was happening for an eternity. Div stood in the doorway looking on, there but not there. His eyes were glazed. Shock. Medication. The doorbell finally rang. Mum screamed at Div to go and answer the door. He made his way downstairs, slowly, on crutches. The ambulance crew arrived and thought the call was for Div until they heard the commotion upstairs. Mum cleared out the room. I was left in the room with the ambulance woman. She asked me to help lift Dad from the bed to the floor. It's amazing where strength comes from when you need it. We lifted him to the floor easily. They got out their equipment and tried to shock him. It looked very scary. It looked like it was on TV not in our house, not to my dad. They tried again to shock him. Nothing. Then again. They looked at us and apologised with the words, "I'm afraid he's gone". Gone. Gone…? How could he be gone? He'd had a huge heart attack. Me, Mum and Div looked at each other. One minute we were crying, then we were hysterically laughing, then we were hugging. We didn't know what to do with ourselves. It was the longest night ever. The ambulance crew waited for the police to arrive. The police had to arrive as it was a sudden death. Then we had to wait for the doctor to arrive to declare the death. Then a neighbour friend arrived to sit with Mum. Then we had to wait for the undertaker. There were people in and out of the house all night. All that was going over and over in my mind was *where's my daddy gone?*

A NEW BEGINNING

A fter Dad died, I guess I just decided to continue and move forward. I'd already handed in my notice although I took my last month off work due to what had happened. I went back on my last day which happened to be the last day before the Christmas break. We went to the pub at lunchtime. There were drinks about on desks when we got back to work. I remember a particularly strong vodka being poured for me as it was my last day. The team was great with me and my manager, aka BFG (Big Fat Gordy), was a superstar. I'd let him down by just upping and leaving but he knew what I was going through and was very good to me. He had met my dad earlier that year at my twenty-first birthday party. The drinks were flowing, and we went out from work to the pub next door. I was knocking back a right old mixture. I'd been on the vodka, I had a few pints, a pint of Guinness, some shots then vodka jelly. Everyone was remarking on how sober I seemed. I guess it was just down to the shock of everything recently. We had a nice time. I think I needed it after all that had happened, so I really let my hair down. We left the pub and I hit the cold air. Literally in that instant I was legless. What is it with cold air that does that? I went from being the life and soul of the party to being an absolute mess. Two of the boys from work had an arm around each side of me trying to get me down the street. I woke the next morning and opened my hurting eyes. Oh shit, where was I? I was in bed. Oh crap, it looked like a boy's room. I looked on the side and there were a few pints of water. There was a sick bowl on the floor. My hair was stuck to my face with sick. I slowly rolled over dreading to see who was beside me in the bed, in the room where I had no idea where I was. I slowly rolled over and, thank fuck, there was no one else in the bed. I had on some clothes. My lenses were not in my eyes, so everything was extra blurry. There were some flashbacks. Me puking against a pub window and my boss walking past and laughing, some coffee. The police. Why were the police there? A boy's face. I remember a boy's face, but it was upside-down. Shit, this was bad. I didn't know where I was. I was mingingly hungover and I felt like shit. I was scared. My phone was nearby. I took a guess as to where I was which was hard due to my head being so fuzzy. I guessed I may have still been in Epsom, one of my work colleagues lived there. I picked up the phone and called him. He answered bright and breezy and told me to come out of the room and turn right. Thank fuck, I was in his house. This was one of my first blackouts. Mikey had slept on the settee and was still wrapped in a duvet when I made a feeble entrance. He was smiling and asked how I felt. I felt sodding awful. He asked if I remembered anything, well no, I didn't remember much apart from the police. He said they struggled to get me down the road as I was paralytic. I threw up right outside a big pub window, so all the pub saw and were laughing at me. My boss walked past, saw the funny side, and went to get me a coffee. I don't think I could drink it. They tried to get me back to the house, Mikey's, to sleep it off. Mikey got my phone from my bag and did the decent thing and called my mum to let her know I wouldn't be able to travel back, and he would put me up for the night. They couldn't move me very much as I was a dead weight. The police stopped them as there were two men dragging a completely drunk girl along the street. They asked the police for help and if they could drive me to Mikey's flat which was only a few minutes away, but the police refused and left us all. They eventually managed to drag me back. Mikey's flatmate was there and helped as I was carried up the stairs, the face I could remember but I was upside-down as I was over someone's shoulder. Apparently, I was complaining to Mikey that I couldn't sleep in my contact lenses, so he got them out for me - yuck. I threw up in a bucket he held for me while I was in bed. Thank God I worked with such nice people that were willing to help me. It could've been much worse. Then Mikey drove me all the way back to Mums the next morning. Mum just smiled and shook her head when she opened the door as I guess she knew I'd been through it lately, as had she. The blackout was so scary. Once they start to take place, they only get worse. At this time when people started to remind me of what happened things gradually started to come back, hazily, but I had some recollection. Later, I would learn that it didn't matter how much I was reminded of what had happened, once it had gone it had gone. I don't know if this is a blessing or a curse. Either way, blackouts are bloody awful, and I'm still left with some gaping black holes of not remembering a thing. As time went on, I was left with more and more of them.

LIFE AT A HOLIDAY VILLAGE

I'd left my job. I packed all my belongings and loaded up my car. I drove to the Isle of Wight on my own which was an achievement in itself. I don't remember saying my goodbyes. As there seemed to be so much going on it went by in a bit of a blur. It was new beginnings for me. I was excited, I was sad. My mind had been made up though so that was the hardest part done. Now it was time to move forward and get on with life. Start a new life with Dean. It was crazy, I still had to pinch myself to check it was really happening. There had been enough doom and gloom, so it was time to get excited and I was excited. I finally arrived. Dean was sharing a huge flat with friends, a married couple and a lodger. I knocked on the door expecting Dean to rush and greet me with excitement. Kat answered the door and welcomed me. She told me Dean was in the bedroom. I went to the bedroom to make my entrance. He was lying on the bed, watching telly. He didn't even look up when he said hi. The biggest alarm bell went off in my head. I'd changed my fucking life around and just been through hell and he couldn't even be bothered to look up from the telly to acknowledge me. I didn't let it show. I started unloading my car, I don't think he rushed to help me.

Dean was working in pubs after leaving the Savoy. Obviously, this involved pub hours, so he was out most evenings and during the days, and I was left to find my own way. I started looking for jobs, but it was the Isle of Wight. I stupidly thought it would be easy to pick up an IT job with the four years' experience I had but they didn't seem to have those type of jobs on the Island. It was mainly seasonal work in catering or cleaning. I kept looking but there was literally nothing. I spent most of my time at Savoy and by then had a wide group of friends who worked there. As I never did the uni thing I guess I never had a chance to let my hair down after finishing school and this is the time I started doing that, big time. I was there all day, in and out of friends' chalets and the bar, following on to being there all evening. Kat was a manager there and ended up getting me a job in the gift shop as she knew I wasn't having any joy with the job searches so thought it would help. I'd gone from IT to a gift shop, but I was going to make the most of it and I was enjoying life to the fullest. I barely saw Dean as our shifts overlapped.

In no time, Dean and I were engaged. He went on a trip to South Africa where he bought the ring and proposed shortly after he arrived back. I kind of knew the proposal was happening but I wasn't meant to. We were going out to lunch at a friend's restaurant and he was suited and booted. Kat asked if he 'had everything' before he left which was a bit of a giveaway. We were still at the awkward silence stage and really didn't know each other very well, even though I'd changed my life to be with him. I nipped to the loo after lunch and on the way out of the toilet, everyone was looking at me. Everyone meaning the owner of the restaurant, Dean, and two older ladies that were sitting a few tables down from us. When I got back to the table, he got down on one knee and proposed. I said yes. I wasn't into being in the spotlight, so I was embarrassed and still a little in shock, even though I knew it was coming. I was really pleased and excited, but I think we both saw our relationship through rose-tinted glasses. We then went to the pub across the road in Yarmouth and people were handing us congratulations cards, so it seemed most people knew before me.

Hindsight is a wonderful thing and it probably wasn't either of our wisest decisions. We weren't seeing much of each other and when we did, we didn't have anything to say. I remember Dean finishing a lunch shift and calling me, I was at the holiday village as usual, and he asked me to go back home so we could spend some time together. When I got home, he complained of never seeing me then went to bed and fell asleep, pot kettle sprang to mind. We gradually drifted apart although we hadn't really been together. At some point, Kat's sister came from South Africa to stay for a long break so there were six of us in the flat. Dean and I went on a short break away. We called it all off whilst waiting for the Eurostar to go for a romantic break to Paris and then had to spend the weekend away together. It was all a bit of a non-event. We thought it was meant to be, but it was just a holiday romance. We didn't have much in common and still acted like strangers, so it seemed the best idea. It was upsetting, all breakups are, but we knew we had to do it as it couldn't continue as it was as there just was no relationship. I didn't have anywhere else to live so for a few weeks I stayed at the flat but slept in the front room on the sofa bed with Kat's sister. It was all a bit hectic, but my life was hectic back then and hectic became the norm.

I was working in reception and the shop and at times covered the dishwash, worked in the still room, on housekeeping and on baby listening. I picked up whatever shift I could get. Shortly after my breakup with Dean, I'd started seeing someone else. I had to leave the flat as it really wasn't convenient living with an ex and sharing a bed with another friend, so I pretty much moved in with the new boyfriend straight away. It only seemed like we'd met for a few minutes and then I was living with him on site. We were all on minimum wage and the board and food were taken out of the pay, so we earnt little over £100 a week but that was just beer money. When my shift finished, I'd be straight to the bar until that closed, then start in the shop the following morning at 8 a.m. By then my life was one-hundred per cent holiday camp. I don't know how my body survived it as I was drinking every night. My one season turned into a whole four years and I think I can count on one hand the days I went with no alcohol in the time I was there. I had become part of the furniture.

I could see the shop and reception from my bedroom window and the bar was about a twenty second walk from the mouldy shed that was my chalet. I'd struggle out of bed, my head pounding, shove my hair back and put some makeup on to try and cover the bags. I'd then stick my glasses on to try and cover most of the damage, throw up if necessary, brush my teeth, and get to work. The first job was getting the papers set up which involved lugging heavy newspapers into the shop, sitting on the floor putting the inserts in then getting them on the shelves before the shop opened. The lifting was the worst part for me as by this time there wasn't a day that went past where I didn't feel horrifically hungover. I'd be really short of breath and my heart would be pounding and I was always aware of my breathing, it was like if I didn't give it any thought it would stop entirely. I must've still stunk of drink from the night before, but I used to plough on through. I'd crave sugar so would load up on Lucozade and chocolate but sometimes that would get thrown straight back up. Then I'd feel like I needed something savoury to make me feel better so I would phone one of the waiters and ask them to bring me over some breakfast. The fry ups didn't always make it to the shop as bits of food would literally slide off the plate due to all the grease it was swimming in. Then I'd feel awful and some days that would also come back up. It wasn't just the top half either, I had real grog-bog due to all the alcohol and it wasn't pleasant, but I won't go into details. Then I'd crave something sweet again and I'd try to drink as much water as possible. In general, apart from all the water, my diet was shocking. I was trying to self-medicate the hangover by food and nothing worked. I couldn't even sleep in my breaks as I felt too awful and was too aware of my breathing to be able to relax. I used to sit at the till with the doors wide open, shivering, but I had to stay awake. The tiredness was dreadful, and I was literally nearly asleep on my feet. A typical day would be finishing up in the shop then starting a shift in reception until 6 p.m. I used to like talking to people in reception and giving advice on the places to visit or eat at. I decided to be a proper tourist during my time on the Island and went to most of the attractions. I'd got hold of the Isle of Wight pub guide that had 171 pubs listed. My aim was to visit them all and I ticked off all bar two, so I was a font of all knowledge when it came to pubs and attractions. I read most of the books there were regarding the Island and particularly liked the ghost books and collected them all. The Isle of Wight Tours manager used to joke and ask me to join them as I knew so much of the history of the Island. If you needed advice or some history, then I was the man. However, chatting to people and being friendly isn't great when you are suffering from the worst hangover you think it's possible to have and just standing upright becomes a complete mission. Somehow, I managed it though and would always vow never again.

After my shift, if I wasn't on baby listening, I'd be out the door straight home to shower and change and hurry to the bar. I'd head there for a hair of the dog and after a couple of pints I'd start to feel human again. I always had every intention of stopping at the point of normalising myself, but it never happened and then I'd go on the wine, have a few shots and before I knew it, it would be about 1 a.m. and I'd be pissed as a fart. I'd get back to my shed, sometimes throw up, and get in bed with walls spinning until the next day when it started all over again. I seriously don't know how my body coped. I was really pushing it and even without a drink I was exhausted and shouldn't have been able to push through and keep it up. At one point I was also working as a waitress at a local restaurant so was working even more hours. My feet would be so sore from standing all day and night and it felt like the only thing I could rely on was a drink or two to get me through until the shift finished. I was dead on my feet. In between feeling constantly shit throughout the days I thoroughly enjoyed myself. Some would say too much. My savings had long gone, and I was just earning beer money while I was living there. I didn't really care much at the time. I always thought it would be my last season so make the most of it, but it turned into four years of serious abuse to my poor body and mind.

When the site was no more it left a gaping hole in my life. It was bought out and was turned into owners' cottages. In a way I guess I was relieved that I wouldn't have to put my body through all that anymore, but this was just the beginning of my problems.

ANOTHER MOVE

I t was a really sad time. Not only had my favourite holiday place gone but it had also become my life. I lived, worked, and breathed Savoy. It was in my blood and I didn't really know what hit me when it was no more. My boyfriend and I had found a cottage to rent nearby in Freshwater. It was a lovely little cottage and I thought it would be great for a new start. We also inherited a cat who came with the cottage as he wasn't keen to leave. That was great for me as we'd always had cats in our household and I was a bit, and still am, of a crazy cat lady. My boyfriend was doing bar work so was out most evenings which was fine by me as we weren't particularly getting on. I was on my own and drinking, trying to fill the void. At the back of my mind I knew it was an issue, but I never could admit it to myself and convinced myself I was having a relaxing drink at home. It'd start off with a few beers and a bottle of wine but to be honest I don't really know what I was drinking around that time. I used to hide bottles and cans while my boyfriend was at work, not all of them, as far as he was concerned, I was a normal drinker. If there were too many, I'd decide to hide them under drawers in the bedroom until I could creep them into the bin without him noticing the amount I'd been drinking. This backfired when he decided to move the bedroom furniture around and found a stash of empties which I couldn't explain away. During our four years together, we had also got engaged. There is a lovely place on the Island called Culver. During our pub searches to tick off in the guide, we came across a pub right at the top of Culver Down. From there you can see about three quarters of the Island and all the shoreline and it's beautiful. I decided it was one of my favourite places on my favourite island so one evening, out of the blue, my boyfriend decided to take me there. This was back at the time we were living on site. I knew something was up and kind of knew what was coming so tried to talk him out of it, saying I didn't fancy a drive, but he was adamant. Sure enough, we reached the top and he got down on one knee with a ring. "I'll think about it", was the reply I gave. Clearly, if you have to think then it's a no but he wasn't having it. He kept pushing for an answer in the car on the journey back and was getting angry. I told him to stop at a pub so I could have a drink, a fag, and a think. Instead, I found the nearest fruity and had a gamble, a drink, and a fag, while he sat stewing for an answer. I could've done the grown-up thing and been honest, but I was in my early twenties and although it was a no from me, I didn't have the guts to tell him. In the end, I just said yes as I felt bad for him, but I never had any intention of going through with the marriage. I was engaged for the second time, this time with my third long-term(ish) boyfriend that I didn't want to be with from the off. The only one I had really cared about had been Dean but that didn't end up as I had imagined so I just went along with it.

I was lost without the Savoy and was filling the void with drink and cat cuddles. I still had mates, but it wasn't like the old days where you could just turn up at someone's room at any time in the night and be welcome. Old friends used to turn up and pop in, but I still felt very lonely. I had managed to get a job, this time next door to the Savoy at Warner Holidays. I'd only been there a couple of weeks and was getting on well. I used to turn up for work and drive home without visiting the bar, which was a rarity, although I always managed to stop at the offy on the way home. Every time I got a sale for a holiday, I earned myself a £10 voucher which could be spent in several places, one of them being Threshers. I earned more in vouchers than I did in salary per week. Guess where all those vouchers were spent? During this time my then-fiancé and I split up. I will call it a messy breakup, which it was, and my life was utter chaos for a few weeks. One night, Maca and another friend from Savoy popped in and asked if I wanted to go for a drink in the social club, or anti-social club as it was known. I was on my own and half pissed and thought why not. I've not mentioned Maca yet. He used to work at Savoy and I always had a soft spot for him. He was a little weird but in a quirky way, not creepy-weird. The main thing was he made me laugh from the first moment I met him. I always found him a little awkward but that could have been because I fancied him. Later I found out he felt the same way so there was always a little bit of tension. On the spot, I decided I would join them down the anti-social. I can't really remember it and I was pretty far gone with the drink, but it was nice to feel free. Maca walked me back to the cottage and we ended up kissing. Like all my previous relationships, I moved straight into the next one without really knowing how it happened but this time I was a lot happier with Maca. The big difference this time was that we were the best of friends.

CONTRACTS

Maca and I were together for four or five years, maybe even six. This is where my drinking took a real turn for the worse, so I have no real idea of how things happened or in what order. I want to point out my drinking was nothing to do with him, my drinking was purely because I was an alcoholic. I'll do my best to explain but if it seems sporadic and bitty that's because it was. I have no real recollection of about ten years of my life. Sometimes when I'm talking, I'll refer the 2000s as the 1990s. This is because I literally lost about a decade, it all spun past in a hectic blur of complete and utter chaos.

Maca got a job in Southampton. He asked if I wanted to go with him. I really loved him then despite the hazy alcohol head I had. I was with someone I really cared for, I just didn't have a great way of showing it. We rented a one-bedroom ground floor flat in Hedge End. During this time, I was polishing off at least a bottle of wine an evening which progressed to drinking constantly throughout the day. I somehow managed to get back into IT support as a contractor. I'd been out of IT for about five years due to the 'short' career break I took, so it was difficult at first. I just needed to get that first contract. The job began with about twenty of us supporting one rollout of a new system. The drill was, as soon as the calls started dying down then they would have to start getting rid of people. I was working hard and getting on well. I was drinking but was in some kind of control, if you can call it that. Occasionally I'd be hungover and would have to struggle on until the evening so I could have my fix. I think I missed the first two out of three days of training due to alcohol withdrawal but after that I decided to try my hardest. We were covering a twenty-four-hour shift and I was mainly on the early shift, 7 a.m. - 3 p.m., as that was the busiest. I'd cover the occasional evening or night. One evening I was drinking, and I was doing it at my desk. We were a close-knit team and during the night there was barely any work to do so we used to play board games together or take quizzes. The others sussed something as while I was sitting in my car in the pitch black during my break, after driving to the nearest shop for wine, I heard a tap on my window. It was my team leader who asked me what I was doing. I can't remember what I said. They knew I was drinking as I'd left an empty Sprite bottle on my desk which had been full of some kind of booze. A Sprite bottle was my bottle of choice, it's green so you couldn't see exactly what was in it, therefore doing a good job hiding my chosen alcoholic drink. Due to my weird behaviour, they put two and two together and smelt the bottle. I couldn't deny it, I was caught red-handed. I remember there being tears and me telling them I was sorting it, but I didn't lose my job as I had expected. I was very humiliated though and it was one of the first times I had to admit to having a problem, even though I still didn't think

I had one at the time. The staff gradually got whittled down, worst went first, and I was one of the last of the remaining. There were about four of us left and I was offered a permanent job. I believe this offer happened on a Friday, but I'd already picked up a contract starting the following Monday, as I was expecting my current contract to end. I decided to take on the new job as it was slightly more money, but I would later very much regret that.

I started the new job the following Monday, still in two minds as to whether I should have gone to a permanent position in the previous role. On my first day, I knew I'd made a mistake. I'd been hammering it that weekend and I'm usually a grafter when it comes to working. No matter what, I would struggle through and previously had a track record of working hard. On the first morning I turned up late. I'd been drinking on the way in, driving I must add, which was ridiculous no matter what way you look at it. I thought I was fine though and believed it. I'd poured some alcohol, I can't remember what type, into the usual Sprite bottle whilst in the car park. I'd spilt a load in my lap so on my first day I turned up late, stinking of booze, and looking like I'd peed myself. This job was the most boring I've ever had. I was an IT administrator, but this was code for the manager wanting some kind of glorified secretary to up his status but having no actual work for me. I literally had no work. I was in an open plan office with a team of developers. I struggled to fit in. The office was pretty much silent all day and I used to write on a piece of paper how long in minutes I had to go until my shift finished. I was constantly asking for work, but they had nada. Some days I would get in my car and cry with relief during the journey home as I hated it there so much. My drinking was worse, and I was pretty much drinking throughout, trying to stabilise myself to sobriety by medicating drink. It's really hard work being an alcoholic. You have to have exactly the right amount at the right time to be able to feel normal. Any more and you get far too pissed almost instantly from the constant topping up, and any less you land up feeling totally shit with serious anxiety. My mood was up and down, emotions high then low, I was happy and sad, it seemed to all happen at once. The team went to the pub one lunchtime and I tagged along. I had one or two pints of cider and was legless. They must've thought I couldn't handle my drink, but I'd topped up that bit too far and gone to the seriously pissed stage. I tried to get to the car park to hide in my car, but someone managed to find me and take me back to work for some coffee. The room was spinning, and I had to see the day out. I couldn't even walk. The following Monday I sent an email round to the team telling them some bullshit about how I shouldn't drink on medication (I wasn't on any) and that I was sorry if I offended anyone. A few weeks later I literally nodded off at my desk. My colleague sitting next to me got the boss and I was summoned. I sat in a room with my boss and the guy from HR that employed me whilst being told they had reason to believe I was drinking at work. I denied it, looking them straight in the eye, pissed. My ID badge was taken from me and I was escorted from the premises. The humiliation and shame were in me somewhere, but I was too relieved to notice.

I picked up another IT contract. Just before this, I'd spoken to the agent whilst having a breakdown, telling him that I couldn't work as I was dependent on alcohol. I'd been in and out of doctors' surgeries and was actually classed as alcohol dependent. During my episode of meltdown, I told the agent everything. Much to my surprise, he called me back after speaking to the company that had just hired me and told me they were still willing to give me a try, if I could sort myself out for the Monday. They believed everyone deserves a chance. I couldn't believe there were such nice people about and really sorted myself out for the start of the new job. The first week, even though a little uncomfortable knowing that the management knew, went well. I was enjoying being back at work and I think I had managed to control the drinking a bit. I can't really remember but I was making it to work and was happy so that suggests I'd controlled in some form, I think I didn't touch it at all, but I can't remember. During my second week, on the Thursday night I'd had too many and had to find a hair of the dog at lunchtime the following Friday. I did my Sprite bottle trick then got a bit lairy at my desk. Seeing the change in personality and putting two and two together, my boss checked the bottle I'd stupidly left in the bin and sure enough, it stunk of wine. The following Monday I was called into his office and in the middle of the desk sat my empty Sprite bottle. I already felt like shit, on yet another comedown, and knew what was coming. I sat there in tears and told him it had my medication in it, and he said he'd never known any medication smelling exactly like wine. It wasn't really a lie as the wine was my medication at the time, it was the only thing that helped me to feel human again. He was upset too and said he'd been speaking to his wife about it the night before as he really wanted to give me another chance but couldn't. I held no grudges, they'd given me a chance and I'd blown it. I was sacked again.

HOMELIFE

I picked up some more contracts but if I wasn't sacked, I think I left them. I was out of my mind. I don't know how poor Maca put up with me for so long. He knew I wasn't a bad person just that I had issues, I definitely had a few of those. The drinking was spiralling. I can't tell you an average day of drink because I have no idea. How could I measure it when it was throughout the day and when I woke up feeling awful at night? It was a constant twenty-four-hour battle for the booze. Maca knew I drunk, he'd see the bottle of wine of an evening, but it was far more than that. It was stashed around in every nook and cranny I could find in that flat. Sometimes I'd hide it so well even I couldn't find it which was hideously frustrating. Some nights the night sweats and shakes would be so awful that I'd already have a bottle of vodka hidden under my pillow, just in case. The smell of the sweat was toxic, and I don't know how Maca shared a room with me, let alone a bed. I would sweat through the duvet and be so hot I'd feel like I was about to spontaneously combust. I'd move an inch and be frozen on the spot. This used to happen throughout, so I was constantly wriggling about trying to get the temperature right. The only thing that would settle it would be another drink, but that next drink would only make it worse when that started wearing off. It was a vicious circle and the control was taking over. Maca would go to work and I'd be straight out the flat, walking into town to get my next fix. I'd always try to keep a bit of drink back to get me through the walk, but some nights were so unbearable I'd end up drinking it during the night. I would have to orientate my way, my breathing laboured, anxiety at its peak, just to get to the shop. There were about three shops in the area that sold booze and I was always switching up my shops so that I wasn't recognised multiple times a day buying it. I'd also add other bits to my shopping basket just so it looked like I wasn't there to buy alcohol at 8 a.m. when you were able to buy your first. It was utter madness.

My days consisted of drinking and conking out. Maybe a bit of tidying and a shower, always a shower, I still had some pride. I couldn't always manage makeup or housework, but I tried. I'd put music on and play the same things over and over while my emotions were erratic. One minute I'd have Black Lace blaring out while I was doing party dances, clearly I was still missing holiday camps, and the next moment I'd be listening to something that made me cry. Then I'd be conked out somewhere sleeping. I'd wake feeling shit so start all over again. Each time I'd think I had enough drink to get me through the day, but some days I was out maybe four times to get a fresh supply. The evening drink of wine in front of Maca would be draining low and I'd physically feel the fear creeping in, wondering how I was going to cope during the night or the following morning. I'd be desperately trying to remember if I'd stashed some anywhere. Maca guessed how much I was drinking and our recycle bin was always overflowing with bottles, even though the majority of them I used to lose on the way to the shops. Our relationship was strained and we'd have huge arguments, always started by me, followed by tears and accusations. I was always accusing him of being with someone behind my back as it was a real fear of mine. I don't think he ever actually did although if he did, I'd never blame him, he was living with a crazed nutter. He'd stick by me and I'd always complain of feeling fluey in the mornings, saying I thought I was coming down with something. He just never commented. He wasn't stupid so I don't know why I thought I'd take him for an idiot. I did feel fluey, I could barely get out of bed. The nightmares were starting and sometimes I'd wonder if I was dreaming or awake. My life was one big nightmare and I was dragging him down with me. Money was tight but I always found a way to get my alcohol fix whether it be beg, borrow, or steal. Maca and Mum bailed me out loads. Mum knew things weren't good, but I don't think she understood how bad it had got as I was so far away. She could tell on the phone by my voice how pissed I was, but I just used to fob it off.

My rages were getting worse. One night when Maca got home I was accusing him of all sorts. I was so scared he was going to leave me but instead of being nice to him and treating him well I just seemed to push him away. My rage was so bad that I punched the wall several times. The wall I'm referring to was about an inch in between two door frames separating our kitchen and bedroom, so it wasn't a flat surface. I knew instantly I'd done something to my hand but kept punching. The pain was bad even though I'd had plenty to drink and was pretty numb. I was working another contract, back on a service desk. I'm a touch-typist and I remember the pain when I'd use my little finger on my right hand. My hand had swollen, and you couldn't see my knuckles. It was three days later when my boss noticed. I told him I'd had a row and punched a door frame and he saw the funny side and offered to drive me to the hospital at lunchtime. Instead he drove me to the pub! I didn't see that one coming. I had an inkling that he fancied me, and I think he was trying his luck. He ordered a coke so I couldn't order anything alcoholic even though it was killing me sitting in a pub with a coke, it was unheard of. He was married with kids, but I know a player when I see one and he was testing the water. I gave off no vibe, other than the not interested vibe, and we went back to work. I decided to get my hand checked out after work and ended up with it plastered and in a sling. I'd broken my little finger. It still gives me a bit of jip now when it gets cold. I left the hospital, took off the sling and drove home with my hand in plaster. I never got the plaster removed or the bone rechecked at the hospital. The cast was starting to smell so horrendous from all the night sweats that it would wake Maca up in the night. I would be constantly rubbing hand gel down the sides, but the stinking cheese smell it emitted was pretty grim. I couldn't wait six weeks to get that thing off, it was making me throw up when I didn't feel great, so I took a pair of kitchen scissors to it which was the biggest relief. It also meant I was able to wash my hair again which after a night of sweats didn't leave it very nice. Maca had been washing it for me for weeks, bless him.

One night was really dark and depressing. We were arguing and no doubt I was accusing Maca of something he hadn't done. I was in a state and had been drinking non-stop for weeks. I was in a rage and was suffering from alcohol induced depression. He was on the brink of leaving me. How he'd stayed with me for as long as he did was nothing less than a miracle. I didn't know how I could get him to stay. To make him stay my drink-fuelled illogical mind told me to go to the kitchen and get the biggest kitchen knife I could find. He didn't know what I was going to do. I didn't know what I was going to do. I went to the bathroom directly opposite the kitchen and sat on the toilet seat in my underwear. To make him stay, my insane head told me to start cutting myself. I took the knife to my thigh and started crisscrossing cuts in my leg. The blood was oozing out in perfect lines, I was creating a grid on my leg. I don't know what I was doing at the time, it was like I was possessed by alcohol. Maca froze for a moment then tried to get the knife from me. He had to be careful as he didn't know where my mood would take me, and he must've been petrified that I was going to stab him. Instead I stabbed myself. The knife sunk deep and the blood pumped out. I've always been really scared of blood and the sight of it can make me feel faint but right then I was numb. I wasn't feeling any pain, I wasn't feeling anything. I had no feelings left. I saw the blood and Maca's utter shock, so I did it again, the second time harder and deeper. I hit bone and the blood literally spurted out and hit the wall. Maca was shouting, I was in a trance, there was a lot of blood, a lot. In the end he managed to take the knife from me and was panicking. I stayed motionless looking at my leg and the mess. I had two gaping holes where I could see tissue and I think bone; all sorts were poking out. The bathroom was splattered with blood, all up the walls and oozing onto the floor. Maca had recently taken a first aid course at work. I think he was in shock. He grabbed a first aid box from somewhere and started to clean me up. He pinched the skin together while he stuck it, then rushed me to the hospital. He was in a panic. I, on the other hand, was calm as anything, completely numb. I saw the triage nurse and told her I'd stabbed myself and I was dependent on alcohol. She looked at my leg and then looked me in the eyes and said, "You poor thing". I was shocked. No one had ever said anything like that before. What I was used to was being judged and told to stop or given some useless advice. It was the first time someone, who wasn't family or Maca, showed they genuinely seemed to care. This shocked me more than what I had done to my leg. I was used to the poor me feeling but in a *poor me, pour me another one* way. In the waiting room Maca and I had another row and he went to wait in the car. I waited for another hour or so, but I wasn't seen so I walked out and back to the car. When Maca realised I hadn't waited to be seen he was fuming. No doubt I was in a rush to get back to my precious alcohol. We drove home and the next morning I woke after a fretful sleep with a dragging feeling in my right leg. It felt bruised and throbbed each time I took a step. The wound looked nasty. There were yellow bits of fatty tissue poking out the gaping hole. It really wasn't pretty. Maca cleaned it up and taped it together again.

I didn't get my leg looked at until a few days later when I decided to go to a walk-in clinic, I limped in instead. It was far too late for stitching, so they did the same and cleaned it up and dressed it. It was ignorant of me, but I didn't realise the femoral artery was so close to where I had stabbed. The repercussions this could have had is more than shocking, no wonder Maca looked so worried at the time. I'm now left with two scars which look exactly like they are, stab wounds. It's a reminder of where I've come from. When I tan you can see the criss-crosses.

There were so many more incidents and rows and utter chaos but it's all a bit of a blur. At one time Maca packed up his car to leave me, his mate from work was there to help him. I was begging him not to leave and causing a scene in the car park, but he remained firm and said he'd made up his mind. His golf clubs were nearby waiting to be packed into the boot. I picked one up and was swinging it around at him and his mate. To stop him going I ended up putting the club through his windscreen so he couldn't drive that night. Instead, his mate drove him away in his car.

Maca moved back to his family home on the Isle of Wight and I was left in Southampton with no job and feeling totally alone. He'd taken all his things, so I was left with a bedroom with a bed in it and a front room with a sofa bed in it, nothing else. I hadn't many belonging as any spare cash I had went on booze. There was probably no food in the flat. I remember breaking down looking around an empty room, I didn't have so much as a book to read.

We were on and off but somehow, I always managed to get him back. I don't know if he came back out of love, pity, or worry, but we lasted another few years. We ended up moving back to Mum's, but it was very strained. Div was living at home and his girlfriend had also moved in. My drinking was up and down, maybe a bit steadier at times but still constant. Mum didn't know what to do with me and there were plenty of arguments. I was stealing money from wherever I could find it in the house and was in a drunken stupor most of the time.

After a while we all had a big bust up and we fell out with Mum. Maca and I had been out somewhere and had a row in the street on the way home. The police were passing and tried to break up the argument and Maca had the hump and went back to Mum's. Mum was fuming at him for leaving me out on my own knowing I was off my head but on this night Maca had also had too much to drink and I think he just lost it, after years of shit from me. He and Mum had an argument while I was in the high street looking for a friend of mine. I found him in the local pub, and I think I managed to get myself barred. I'd lost a heel off my boot and I had a big rip down my coat. My friend got me in a cab and took me home where I found Maca on the doorstep. Mum told us we were moving out the next morning.

NORFOLK

I woke with an awful head and that feeling of dread in me but not knowing why until things started to piece back together in my mind and reality began to kick in. My Grandad had passed away a few years previously and, as my dad was no longer around, he had changed his will so that my dad's share was split between me and Div. This happened while I was working at the Savoy. Luckily, we invested the money in property and had bought a one-bedroomed flat in Gorleston, Norfolk, which we had been renting out. It so happened that the tenant was leaving which left the flat free, so we packed the car and Maca drove to Norfolk. This was completely out of the blue and we had no plans.

I hadn't seen the flat before even though I half-owned it as I was probably too busy drinking while Mum and Div sorted it. The tenant wasn't fully moved out, so we had to stay in a B&B for a couple of nights. We couldn't even manage that. When Maca had a drink he really let his hair down and I think he needed it after years of hell with me. On our second night, we'd gone out on the lash and were both legless but were happy together in another new start. Our room was downstairs and when we got in, I fell down the stairs and we caused a commotion. The elderly gentleman that owned the B&B came to the room the following morning and kicked us out. Neither of us had any idea why until he started telling us. I can't remember exactly what we'd done but it was more than me falling down the stairs. We packed up and had to wait in the car in the rain until the flat was ready. I had to get a drink. Maca was so disappointed and upset but was backed into a corner as I was really struggling without one and had long since been diagnosed with dependency. We sat in the car, the rain pouring down, with me swigging from the bottle. The word dependent sounds a bit of a cop out and I'm sure I used it to my advantage at times. It basically means that you can't cold-turkey the drink. Your organs literally become dependent on the alcohol as they are so used to it that they struggle to function without it. Hangovers don't become your standard hangovers, they become withdrawal which is really awful. I was to experience loads more in the coming years.

The flat was lovely and cosy. Maca found work and I struggled. After some time, I found a job and had to drive to Trowse every day, so I needed my wits about me.

ARRESTED

I was working but I shouldn't have been. We'd been out one night, and I'd overdone it and gone past the threshold of being in control. The next morning, I drank on the way to work. I drank at lunchtime and my Sprite bottle made an appearance in the afternoon. On the way home I had to drive down an A road. I'm really not proud of this but I will just tell it as it was. I did have my wits about me in my drink to sobriety way, but clearly, I didn't in the real world. As I was driving the traffic was slowing due to cars joining from a slip road. There was a drastic change in the flow of traffic, and it was slowing nearly to a stop. I was braking but not hard enough. It all went in slow motion. I could see it happen before it happened. I was slamming the brakes. I hadn't been speeding or anything, but I was going into the car in front. I did go into the car in front. My Sprite bottle was in my lap and spilt all over me. The car stopped and I just stopped. I couldn't move due to fear and shock. The lady from the car in front got out and started to walk towards me. She asked if I was OK and I said yes. The police arrived so quickly. I thought this was due to time not functioning normally in my head, but they were actually two cars behind me and had witnessed the whole thing. The policeman was talking to the lady from the other car. I could see an empty wine bottle in the passenger footwell in my car and took the opportunity to throw it out onto the grassy verge at the side of the road. The policeman asked me to step outside of my car and get into the front seat of his. He checked I was OK. I was but I was extra wobbly due to my legs turning to jelly from the shock, not to mention the drink. He said I needed to take a breathalyser test as routine. I told him there was no point, I was over the limit. He saw the bottle on the grass verge and asked if it was mine to which I replied no. He told me it could be fingerprinted so I admitted it was mine. I was sucking furiously on an extra-strong mint hoping it would confuse the breathalyser, whilst necking as much water as I could. He asked me to spit out the mint so it didn't interfere, he was one step ahead of me. I spat out the sweet and had to take the test. I was over the limit, no surprises there. I was instantly arrested and driven to the station. I was chatting away as if it was a usual car journey with a mate. We got to the station and he signed me in, then I was left in a cell. He then called me in for the full breathalyser test. I struggled with this. You have to blow hard for quite a while, and I was feeling breathless from the drink starting to wear off. I tried twice and failed, genuinely. The policeman warned me if I couldn't do it then it would go down as refused, which wouldn't help my case. I tried really hard and managed to finally complete it. The policeman looked at me in shock then told me he had to shake my hand. He shook my hand and said he'd never seen a reading that high with someone seemingly so sober. I blew 126. I think the maximum you are allowed to drive is 35. Oh great,

I was being congratulated on being a functioning alcoholic. In years to come, I was no longer a functioning one.

The night in the cell was hell. There was the usual shouting and cursing noises from other cells, just like you see in the movies. I was freezing cold and I couldn't breathe properly. I was without alcohol and panic was creeping in. When the breathy phases crept in, I'd need a drink to steady it but I was alone and locked up, there was no chance of a drink. The breathing got so laborious that I ended up at the hospital as the police thought it could have been from the seatbelt in the accident. I had to sit in A&E, slightly away from the main waiting area, with two uniformed women officers on each side of me. I wasn't handcuffed as they didn't see me as that much of a threat, but it was very humiliating and people were staring, wondering what I had done. I had an ECG to check my heart whilst the police stayed in the room. I got the all clear and had to go back to the cold cell. My inhibitions were long gone, there was even a camera in the loo. I struggled through the night trying to drink lots of water and peeing it out in front of the camera.

COMMUNITY SERVICE

After a night in a freezing cell, the same policeman knocked on the cell door. I felt like shit and he expected me to after seeing the reading from the previous day. I was offered something to eat but I couldn't face it. I think I managed a cup of tea. We went through for the mugshots and fingerprints then I was let go. I didn't have a penny on me so I had to call Maca and ask if he could pick me up. I had to go to court. The day before the court date, I had to go into Great Yarmouth to meet with my solicitor. I don't remember this at all. I remember sitting in the town centre on a bench, bawling my eyes out, and a stranger stopping to see how I was. I blurted it all out to him and he told me I would be fine. I wasn't fine. I somehow managed to find the solicitor's office but I have no recollection of what happened, this was a blackout and no memory of it has ever returned to me. I was due in court the following morning, yet I was legless. I had to have a drink the next morning to manage to get myself to the court as I was so rough. I saw a sort-of familiar face when I arrived but didn't know where I knew him from. It turned out he was the solicitor I'd met. He said he didn't expect me to remember anything and I couldn't look him in the eye. I'd drunk myself to sobriety again and was feeling shit in every way. The solicitor told me he wouldn't be a solicitor if he was judgemental so ran through some bits with me before the case was heard, but I didn't take any of it in. Maca was with me but he wasn't allowed into the courtroom. I had to stand behind glass and do my bit, ironic as I had a fear of talking in a room full of people. I can't really remember any of it.

I was taken out a different way from the courtroom. Maca was worried as he saw everyone leave but me. I'd already been told I could be getting three months inside as the maximum penalty. He must've been thinking that's what had happened. If Maca had reported the golf club incident then I think I would've gone down but, as it happened, I had no previous. I was escorted to a room where I talked to some kind of official when it dawned on me what I had been sentenced to. I got two-hundred hours of community service and put on probation for a year. I also received an eighteen-month ban so my licence was taken. The licence being taken was a huge relief, I wouldn't have the option of getting in my car over the limit again.

Probation was shit. I had to go into Great Yarmouth once a week at the start to see my probation officer. I don't think I ever went there sober. They knew I had a drinking problem, but I was in between admitting it one minute then pretending I didn't have an issue the next. Eventually, these meetings were reduced to once a month. It was all just a tick box exercise.

Two-hundred hours doesn't seem that much until you break it down to a six-hour day. You are only given one designated day a week. The rule was if you could fit in any other days you can turn up to work, but if there were too many other people there and it was their designated day then you were turned down, but you got an hour knocked off your total for showing willing. On my first day I turned up in my regular clothes, hair done and makeup on not knowing what to expect, and everyone else was in dirty clothes covered in oil. I found out we were to be fixing bikes. I hadn't even ridden a bike since I was a kid, and that was with stabilisers. I've still got scars from riding a bike into a corner of a brick wall, and another from riding too near to a wall where I crushed my finger in the brickwork as a kid. So, fixing bikes was not my forte. I literally have no idea about bike parts. They took one look at my petite frame and lack of bike skills and decided I should be put on an individual placement.

I was put on a placement in a learning centre which was an utter joke. I didn't mind a bit of work so long as it was meaningful work. This place photocopied everything six times for the sake of it and they didn't even need hard copies in the first place. I didn't understand. Some of them were jobsworths but they didn't realise it wasn't really a job, they were just shifting paper from one folder to another and no one needed the paper. I got really bored and the Sprite bottle reappeared. I got so pissed one afternoon and had gone past the getting-away-with-it threshold. I went home saying I was sick, but it was obvious I was pissed. I got kicked off that placement. I think I was the only person there who had been kicked off community service.

I then had to do the real thing with the big boys. I looked so out of place. These were huge, rough looking hard men with tattoos and then there was little me. Sometimes it could be quite fun, if you could call it that. We made what wasn't fun into something not so bad to pass the time. I was getting on with the work and with everyone else. The boys all looked out for me and even the supervisors had a soft spot for me as they could see I just didn't fit in. All the jobs were terrible, but I guess that's the whole point of community service. There was a lot of churchyard work which involved clearing ivy off gravestones, mowing, hedge trimming, strimming and touching up paintwork. At one of the churches we were seen by one of the church-goers who told us what they wanted us to do. After they'd finished someone in the group asked where the toilet was. This person looked at us in utter horror and explained to the supervisor that *those people* could not use their toilet. Ironic as *those people* were doing the dirty work that they didn't want to lift a finger and do themselves. It was just left for *those people* to sort out once a year while no one else kept on top of it.

Other than the churches, one of the main jobs was building a three-mile road through a field - by hand. There were wheelbarrows full of hardcore, to be laid and flattened, all of which I was physically unable to do. I couldn't even lift the wheelbarrow! They'd all be singing, "Hi-ho" and start work while I'd look on and offer to make the tea to make myself useful. The supervisor one day asked if I'd just make tea and clean up after everyone, then worried himself in case I took it as being sexist. I just laughed and was more than happy to do that than the physical work.

Another time we were at a churchyard with a female supervisor. She was also petite but was on a huge power trip. She took a dislike to me so the boys took a dislike to her. It can become very psychological working in a group. Even when we had to meet up with the Crabbies, the Cromer community service group, it was 'us and them' even though we were all in it together. Anyway, we were in a graveyard wheelbarrowing a load of rubbish onto a heap and it was boiling hot as it was summer. I got called to one side and told that I couldn't have my shoulders on show as it was against health and safety that I was wearing a vest top. It was sweltering and all I had with me was a fleece. The supervisor wanted me to wear the fleece to which my argument was health and safety, it was midday in the height of the summer. There was a bit of an argument and I don't think I obeyed (I was a bad girl by then), I just kept hidden behind the huge bonfire pile without my fleece. After the session finished and we were walking back into town she came running out of the centre waving a piece of paper to show me the health and safety rules. I was done for the day and off shift, so I just laughed at her while the boys told her to do one as we were finished. She didn't pick on me after that day, the boys had my back.

I turned up off my head one morning and the supervisors noticed straight away. They had worked out that the drink problem was what had earned me the community service in the first place, and as they were genuinely nice people, they didn't want to make things any worse. They sent me home for the day and said I wasn't fit for work (I wasn't) which was nice of them, but they weren't out to get me in any more trouble than I was already in.

Unfortunately for me, one of the probation officers happened to be popping by at the time and witnessed it. I was summoned back to court, none of which I can remember, maybe because I didn't end up going. I'd breached and was given an extra twenty hours of service.

I still had loads of hours to get through as I had the highest amount out of everyone in my group. Everyone was trying to get the hours down before the winter as a lot of them had previous experience and knew what was to come. The weather changed and it was reed-cutting time. When I say reed-cutting that didn't mean us, they weren't going to allow a bunch of crims loose with cutting tools. We went to some kind of swamp ground, where you could end up knee deep sunken in mud, and we had to move the chopped-down reeds to a bonfire pile. The weather was grim and none of the outdoor-wear fitted me. I had on oversized yellow waterproof trousers and a zip-up coat with hood and looked like I was going to a fancy-dress party as a fisherman. Everything was man-sized so I had to kind of tie and tuck it together. It was cold and wet and the smallest wellies they had were about a size nine - I'm a size four! I had to find a pair I could fit in whilst still wearing my trainers inside, I was a right sight. We had to shovel up the reeds and pile them onto a tarp to then move to the bonfire pile. Every time you moved frogs would jump everywhere and all you could hear from the supervisors all day was, "If anyone throws any more frogs at Vanessa, you'll breach". The boys soon realised that to move the tarp you had to move quickly, or you sunk. They didn't remember to tell me this. I offered to pull one of the four pulleys, so I could muck in, and I grabbed one of the middle ones.

They ran. I was sinking and I couldn't move my oversized boot. The tarp went over my head and I landed face down in the mud. They didn't mean to do it and it was funny, though not really for me at the time. The supervisors were laughing and one of them came to my rescue as I couldn't get up, I was stuck. He managed to lift me but was laughing so much that he also fell, so I was dropped and landed up for a second time face down in the mud.

Another time we were just about to leave a churchyard when the supervisor remembered he had left his keys in the van, locked. He was going to have to call the breakdown service so we could all get home. Some of the boys suggested he went for a fag break. He turned for a couple of seconds and they had that van open with no damage done. The supervisor thanked them, after all he also wanted to get home too, and both he and the boys agreed to not mention it again!

The supervisors were really nice and just trying to keep us out of trouble and they were all very fair. The hardest part of it all for me was getting through the sessions without a drink. I used to get into town as soon as the shops started selling booze to get a couple of miniatures in me to steady the shakes and sweats. I couldn't have too much as I couldn't turn up pissed but had to have enough to stabilise myself. Most of the mornings I spent in Great Yarmouth public loo pouring vodka into a Sprite bottle and necking what I could, having the toilet handy in case anything came straight back up again. I'd get to about lunchtime doing OK but then would start to feel rough and the shakes would creep in. I'd drink plenty of water on the countdown until home time when I could get a proper drink in me, which seemed like eternity. That part was more hard work than the community service itself.

TAMWORTH

At some point, we moved again. This time to Tamworth. Maca's nan had passed away and she'd left the house to him. We were staying there on and off and I was half-heartedly job searching but alcohol had become even more present in my life and I wasn't in any fit state to work. Maca had the whole house redone and we were staying there in the freezing winter with no heating. On the day of his nan's funeral, his mum was also staying in the house. In the morning we started to do some cleaning in the kitchen and clearing out any old food and general rubbish. I started on the cupboards but was really struggling without a drink in me. The shakes had crept in, along with the general demons, and I really wasn't with it and was worried sick about getting a drink. Even though everyone knew I had a problem I was still trying to prove I was a 'normal' drinker so didn't really want Maca's mum seeing me drink in the morning. Then I struck gold. At the back of one of the cupboards in amongst tins long gone past their best-before date I found some spirit bottles. Bingo. I made a 'cup of tea' and my cup was filled with whatever I could find. I ended up going way over my normalise level and was off my head. Apparently, I was in bed talking and shouting to myself while Maca and his mum left for the funeral. I woke up on the ferry going back to the Isle of Wight with no recollection of what had happened. I felt so disrespectful and the shame and guilt were running through my veins, but I couldn't turn back the clock and change anything. I had to sit, very unsteadily, through a ferry crossing trying to swallow down guilt, shame, and puke. No one mentioned what had happened. I think not acknowledging it made it worse, but it was already awful. I wrote a letter to Maca's mum after, apologising and vowing never again. I meant it at the time but didn't stick to my vows.

BACK HOME

Maca and I were on and off and in the end, he finally had to call it a day. He was my rock, my carer, and my punch bag. It just wasn't fair on him. We were both upset but it had to stop. I was back at Mum's, we'd made up long before. I'd been back time and time again over the years so can't remember what time this was. Things got much worse. I managed a few contract jobs but was escorted off the premises at one after drinking half a litre of vodka at lunchtime, topping up from the night before, and was sent home in a cab. I've no recollection of what happened. Ironically, it's the building right next door to where I work now but I can't remember any of the people so I probably pass them in the street daily, I can't even remember what the company was or what my IT job was there. I was incapable of working. It was time I really needed to get some help. I had acknowledged I had a problem. Apparently, or so everyone says, that's the hardest part. I don't necessarily believe that. It was a relief finally coming clean and not having to hide it as much but the shame and guilt that was in me still made me try to hide what I could. Coming clean made it worse in a way because I was still drinking. Once you admit you have a problem people expect you to not drink anymore, so I ended up trying to hide it even more than I had previously.

I managed to control my drinking on and off. That word control again. My life had to be in control, and I had to be in control of my life. I picked up another contract on a service desk and again was doing well. I wasn't teetotal by any means, but I'd got my drinking down and was only really drinking at weekends. This is part of the problem. As I was managing to just drink one bottle of wine on a Friday night and one on a Saturday, I thought I'd conquered my addiction which led me into a false sense of belief. I was in my contract for almost a year which was good going for me. At some point, I had a birthday and decided I'd like a party and Mum agreed we could have one at home as I'd never celebrated my thirtieth. I think on my thirtieth I spent the whole day in bed talking to myself. There always seems to be a semi-heatwave on the week my birthday falls so we had a barbecue in the garden. The next morning, I struggled. I'd had far too much and knew I had to get a hair of the dog inside me as I felt so terrible. I went out the next morning and didn't come back until the early hours of the following morning. I made work on Monday but was still well pissed. I remember trying to find an open shop before work started where I could get my fix and stabilise myself. The stabilising went out the window and I overdid it again. My job was on the phones, not a good job to have when you are slurring and have no idea what you are talking about. I don't really know what happened. I was off my head and the next thing I was aware of was my team leader and boss stood each side of my chair who then escorted me off to another room. I think I had had a fit at my desk. I'd already had a few alcohol-related seizures by this point and knew how I felt afterwards so I put two and two together and I think this is what had happened. They were mainly concerned if I was OK. I was clearly pissed, and I think I told them I had a drinking problem. I left work for the day, and for good, shortly after arriving that morning. It took me about eight or nine hours to get home and I have no recollection of how I made it home, or what happened on the way. I managed to dry myself out again and got back in touch with them. I went in to see one of the big bosses, Pete, and admitted to my problem with alcohol. Amazingly Pete was willing to give me another try. He had put his neck on the line for me and my hard work had paid off. His last words to me were, "Don't let me down". However, I did let him down. I messed up again and turned up drunk, leaving shortly after arriving before I was asked to leave. The management knew what had happened and I wasn't going back this time, I'd already been given a second chance and had failed miserably. I spoke to Pete after and told him how sorry I was, genuinely I was sorry, and couldn't believe what a failure I was to everyone. He was really kind and said he remembered what he had said about not letting him down. He said I hadn't let him down only myself. Didn't I just know it?

At one point I was walking down the local high street, feeling OK but clearly not OK due to having a skinful for breakfast. I walked past the local alky bench where someone was on the floor with an ambulance crew around him. He was refusing to go to the hospital. His mate was trying to talk him around so in my drink-fuzzed head I thought I'd step in to help. It was clear both these men were dependent on drink and the one who wasn't in such a bad way had to take the other back to his flat. My insane head told me to help the sober-ish man drop the not-sober man off to his wife who was fuming but looked used to it. She demanded to know who I was, and I just slurred that I was helping. The other man and I went off drinking somewhere together, I think we even stopped off for an Indian. There was nothing suspect about it although it was mental. You tend to stick around other drinkers to minimise your own problem. We were in the pub and everything was a blur but then realisation dawned on me that I'd just met another alcoholic and gone out drinking with him. I was in the loo at the time and decided I needed to leave without him seeing me. For some reason, I thought I'd escape to the upstairs of the pub. How I thought I'd get out up there I'll never know. I took a step and fell. I managed to fall *up* the stairs. I landed on my face. The bridge of my nose had expertly fallen onto a metal runner that went across the stair where the vertical part met the horizontal. I remember there being a lot of fuss and my 'friend' reappeared alongside a barman holding a damp cloth. They sat me on the step and said I needed to go to the hospital as I'd busted my nose. I felt fine I just wanted to get home. I don't think my nose bled but there was blood from the cut along the bridge of it. I left and got the bus home and fell through the door. I think I announced to Mum that I'd broken my nose and went straight to bed. I woke up the next morning and Mum looked horrified. I said I'd already told her I'd broken my nose, but I guess she was at the point of not believing a word I said as most of what came out of my mouth was nonsense. I took one look in the mirror and knew I was right, it was broken. I had two black eyes and a perfect horizontal cut along the bridge. I couldn't get a doctor's appointment so managed to drag myself to the local walk-in centre. The doctor dismissed me on the spot, I think I must've smelt of booze. I didn't even make it into a consulting room. The receptionist asked if he'd see me and she looked concerned. He took one look said I should've got it looked at when I'd done it and rudely turned me away, to the shock of the receptionist who was very apologetic on his behalf. Luckily my nose didn't end up bent and the scar is now so small you'd struggle to see it, thank God. It did change the shape of my face somehow. I remember I saw Maca at some point after as we still occasionally met, and he couldn't believe how different I looked. He used to joke that my nose was made of concrete as it never moved and yet now, I was able to wiggle it. Another drink induced accident I'd had.

I then picked up yet another service desk contract. Again, I had been sober-ish for a while. I was also in this role for almost a year. Midway through I went off the rails again. I don't think I had drunk at work but there was no point hiding it, I was going to get sacked anyway. I'd had to take time off due to withdrawals, so I spoke to my manager and was let go. I can't remember how or who got in touch first, but I was due to go and see my old manager again a few months later. I'd been clean for a while and was looking much better. Booze used to make my jawline all puffy and my face would have a yellow tinge and I'd look like shit. It used to take at least three months off the alcohol for my face to start morphing back to its old shape and for my skin to improve. I was then nearly glowing and had a spring back in my step and had some hope. I went to meet with my old boss. Another miracle happened and he asked if I'd go back. I jumped at the chance and went back the following week. One thing for sure is people remember who the hard workers are and I've no doubt that if I didn't work hard then I never would have had these second chances. I was back at work and grateful. The rest of the team, bar one, didn't know what had happened and I wasn't ever put in a situation where I needed to explain.

I'd always had an ambition as a teenager to be a glamour model. Ironic as I was so shy. This was my now or never time. I'd sobered up for a good few months and was back working. I decided I was going to go through with it. I was in my early thirties at the time which is nearly retirement age for glamour modelling, but I'd lost so much time already and I didn't want any more regrets. I already had enough regrets of things I had done, I didn't want to start regretting things I hadn't. I was constantly online looking up what I needed to do. I'd never done it, knew no one who had, and I had no idea where to start. I booked my first photo shoot and went for it, my heart pounding. I never had an issue with not having a flat tummy, I got so nervous beforehand I'd spent most of the morning in the loo. I went for the photo shoot and it was like a whole new lease of life. I had a makeup artist and was directed in what kind of shots to take. I loved every moment. I was more pleased than ever with myself. I'd done it and I'd done it alone. Me, who had fear written through my body like a stick of rock, had got out there and done it and I was going to continue until something came of it.

Things at work were going OK up until the work Christmas party. I was friends with one of the guys on the team. I picked up very early on that he was some kind of addict. If you've got it, you spot it. When you suffer from addiction it's pretty easy to spot the ones with the slight nervous disposition and addict attitude to realise. I don't think non-addicts see these small details, but I'd spotted it. I can even tell by the texture of someone's skin. We'd arranged to meet beforehand and to be sober buddies for the evening. It was a posh masquerade do around the corner to where we worked. I arrived in the pub with the rest of the crew, but my non-drinking buddy was nowhere to be seen. He had texted me to say he'd been caught up and was running late. We were at the bar and one of the boys asked me what I wanted to drink. I had a split second to decide and without my ally with me, I chose a white wine. He ordered a large one and the rest of the night was a blur. I could never just have the one and I have no idea how many large ones it turned into. I was off my head. I didn't make it home that night and when my mate finally turned up, he booked a hotel room. I ended up staying there, literally for somewhere to crash for the night. We went on the booze again the next morning together which continued throughout the weekend up until the Sunday night. He was a bit more in control of his drinking and was able to function much better than I was. I was doing so well at work that they'd offered me a permanent role with them. My first day was the following Monday when I was due on my induction as a permanent member of staff, even though I'd been there nearly a year as a contractor. I didn't make it on Monday. They weren't happy with me, and of course, my permanent position was pulled. I can't remember most of that night, but I used to have nightmares of masked people, the last thing I remember from that night. I thought things were at their worst and I'd hit my rock bottom, but then it got really bad.

SICK

I n time, I was by all accounts a non-functioning alcoholic. I couldn't be described as a binge drinker and I couldn't be described as a steady drinker as my drinking was erratic. Some weeks it could be half a bottle of vodka and two bottles of wine a day, and other days a few beers. It was hard to keep track as I was drinking twenty-four hours a day and had it stashed all around for when the nights got so bad. My relationship with Mum and Div was all over the place. Mum ended up my carer for most of it and I can't remember exactly how many years it went on. Each time I suffered a particularly bad withdrawal I promised myself and everyone else never again, and really meant it. Then when I was off it for a week or so I'd feel OK and like I could have a few drinks, but a few was never just a few and I'd be back in a complete mess. Every withdrawal was getting worse each time, though I couldn't believe this was possible. Just a few drinks were totally impossible for me although I kept trying to get back to that normal drinker, each time getting progressively worse. I just couldn't cope without alcohol, even though I couldn't cope with it.

My days consisted of getting up and out as soon as the shops started to sell alcohol. Getting the strongest I could buy with whatever little money I had. If I didn't have money, I'm sorry to admit that I would take it from whoever I could in the household or try to find Mum's or Div's beers and neck them back. I could guzzle a bottle of wine in under five minutes, and that was just to stop the shakes and make me feel human again. I'd long since given up bothering to pour into a glass so it was straight out the bottle. Some days I would raid my penny jar and would go to the shop and shamefully pay for whatever I could with pennies, which was usually a can or two of K cider.

My body didn't know what had hit it. Some days I would projectile puke and the power in which my body rejected the drink was shocking. Sick would spurt out the end of the bed and even hit the cupboard which was against the far wall. I just used to keep drinking until it would stay down. People tell you it's just about willpower and all you need is willpower to stop. Well, it's not that at all. Alcoholics and addicts have willpower and pure determination. It takes a lot of willpower to swallow neat spirits first thing in the morning and to try and keep it down when you know what you are doing is killing you. It takes great determination to drink on, even though your body is physically rejecting it. Why did I keep on? Because I felt like I would die if I stopped and I think that's not far from the truth of what could have happened. I felt as if I'd die if I stopped and die if I continued.

I would have to drink to be able to lift my head off the pillow in the mornings. The nights would be awful, and I'd have a supply to keep me going when the going got really tough. When I'd self-medicated the drink, and only then, was I able to sit upright in bed or be stable enough to get to the bathroom. I mentioned grog-bog earlier and I'm sure most know that your guts aren't too clever after a night on the lash. I can tell you it's much worse when you're on it constantly. When I was finally going, it was nothing less than toxic waste that was coming out of me. My sweats were awful. I looked an utter mess. It was hard to believe that a few months earlier I had been doing photo shoots. I was in hospital again with withdrawal when my photo shoot pictures came through. They'd been sent in the post and Mum brought them to the hospital for me. I was slumped in a hospital bed, an utter mess, looking at pictures struggling to believe it was me. I remember a nurse asking me who they were of.

I was puffy in the face, baggy, and tinged a yellow colour. My eyes were glassy and bloodshot, and my hair was lank with no life. My weight was dropping drastically which was hardly surprising as I wasn't eating. Sometimes I think I went for days without food, I just had no appetite. Mum would force me to eat a dinner which I managed but I couldn't taste anything, it was just fuel to try and keep me alive as I obviously knew I couldn't just starve. I used to be bedbound for weeks on end with Mum nursing me through. I was always told by medical staff that I couldn't cold-turkey, as when I did, I had alcoholic seizures and I knew it could kill me. This was a tough job for Mum. She'd try to work out what I'd had the previous day, which is hard when it's through twenty-four hours solid, and make sure I had less the following day, then less again and so on. This could take a week just to wean me off the stuff, and then I'd still be bedbound for a few days due to being so weak and ill.

The weaning stages were scary for us all. I'd start to feel like I had a seizure coming on which used to panic me and I'd have to have a drink to calm the nerves. I got to the point where I was unable to get out of bed to the toilet next door to my room as I was so dizzy and weak, so I was peeing in a bucket. I used to slip down the edge of the bed using the bed as my back support and pee out pure stinky alcohol. I'd also be puking a lot. The night times were awful, but the days weren't much better. I would have no sleep. Now I know why sleep deprivation was used as torture; it is pure torture. I think the longest I went with not even nodding off once was nearly a week. This plays games with your head. I was awake but felt like I was dreaming. I'd lost any sense of reality. I'd desperately try to sleep but it just wouldn't come. Whenever I closed my eyes I would have horrors and images which would make it impossible to sleep. I was going out of my mind. For someone who when completing IQ tests apparently is in the top 2% of the population, I couldn't believe how stupid I was. I used to lie there and think I had finally gone mad. I couldn't remember the simplest thing. For example, I'd try to remember where I'd get if I turned left or right out of the house and that left me clueless. I'd try to remember people's names who I had sat next to at work and again I'd come up against complete blanks. Occasionally, I'd be able to lay downstairs with a duvet in front of the telly if I could manage to get down the stairs. My legs were like little bird's legs, they were so skinny and weak. I'd lost all my muscle. A few weeks before some of these episodes when I'd been off the drink and trying to be fit, I'd been doing my exercise DVDs, again something I didn't do by halves. I'd have to push myself to do the hardest ones I could find but when I was in this state it was hard to remember how to stand upright without support, let alone jump around doing an aerobics session. I was desperately ill, and I couldn't do anything. The household was strained. One minute we were arguing, then Mum would be begging me to stop, then there would be tears. It didn't matter what was said or what happened, I wasn't getting any better and there was no point with keeping on going over the hows and whys as I was where I was. The sleep deprivation didn't only affect me. Mum had to sleep in with me every night in case I fitted. I had bedsores on my elbows from leaning up to drink. I was also trying to drink loads of water as my thirst was another thing keeping me awake. I knew that dehydration was doing some of the damage both physically and mentally, so throughout the day I'd try to drink as much water as possible, in between the medicated cheap wine. In the night I'd just feel like I was going to drift off, but the thirst would kick in and I'd barely be able to breathe as my throat felt like it was sticking together. Then I'd be propped up on my elbow drinking water at every opportunity. It was a vicious circle night after night. Lay down, have awake nightmares when I closed my eyes, the hot sweats would kick in, I'd move then get a freezing chill. Then get as comfy as possible and my throat would close, and I'd be gasping for water. Drink, then lay back down and it would start again. Then I'd need the bucket for a pee after all the water. On and on this would go, so Mum didn't get any rest either. I really was climbing the walls and seriously thought I'd gone mad.

Eventually, I would drift off to sleep after nights and nights of having none. This would usually be in the mornings after Mum had got up. Apparently, only psychic people dream in colour but, oh boy, my dreams were colourful and psychedelic. I'd be somewhere in a crowd of people. Everyone would be wearing the brightest multi-coloured sequins and there would be shine and sparkle all around, even the rooms would be brightly coloured, so much so that it would hurt my eyes. There would always be vivid faces. Really clear faces but of no one I knew. They would be coming towards me and would all be walking in one direction while I was trying to get through them walking the other way. One dream I remember I was walking on a floating bridge which was moving with the water, it was like walking on a bouncy castle. It was about two metres wide and there were hordes of children everywhere, all walking past me while I was trying to get through them in the other direction. They were all wearing bright clothes and I could see the faces although I knew none. And the singing, the singing was so loud it was making me feel ill. It was a monotonous child's song that repeated over and over again, each time getting louder. I even had the words in my head, but I had never heard the song before, it was something that was created in my dreams. I'd wake up so scared. When I put it down in black and white it doesn't seem scary, but there was something about those nightmares that were so haunting. Mum would look pleased and say I'd finally slept, even though it was for only an hour or so. I'd feel better knowing that my body had got some sleep, but it hardly left me feeling refreshed. When I did have these hour-long awful sleeps, I'd wake up drenched in sweat where I hadn't moved and had just been festering in it.

The seizures were scary for all. I had a fear of fainting and fitting which stemmed from when I was a young teenager, I was probably aged around fourteen or fifteen. I woke one morning and got up a bit quicker than I should have. I opened a drawer to reach for my hairbrush and when it shut, I crushed my finger in it which made me feel sick. I was feeling a bit light-headed so should've sat down but instead I went to the loo, as you do after first waking up. As I walked downstairs, I was getting dizzier and dizzier. I told Mum I was going to either throw up or pass out and she sat me on one of the dining chairs. It was then I fainted, Mum tried to hold me upright in the chair, but I went down, taking the chair with me. I can remember the noise and feeling like I couldn't breathe and that something was stuck in my throat. I came to with Mum on the phone to an ambulance and I was lying on the floor. I looked down and there was blood down the front of my dressing gown. I had had a fit and my tongue had gone back in my throat. No one knew what to do as I was turning blue. My dad's instant reaction was to get my tongue out, so he reached in to try and release it. I had clamped down on his fingers whilst seizuring and bit him badly, hence the blood. Later we found out that I should have just been put in the recovery position with my head held back to release my tongue. I was taken off in an ambulance and kept in hospital for the day while tests were done. They found nothing and put it down to being a teenager and hormones kicking in but said to go back if it happened again. It so happened that a week or so after I was in Camden market and my mate had her nose pierced. As it was pierced it peed out with blood, which I didn't take too well. I fainted and hit the concrete floor landing on my new ear piercing. Then a few weeks after that, I'd woken in the night scratching at my nose due to hay fever, this had given me a nosebleed. I got up to get a tissue too quickly and fainted then too. I went back for more tests, but nothing was ever found. This played a part in my teenage years as it knocked my already low confidence even lower. I couldn't sit in a school assembly as I would imagine myself fitting or fainting in front of the whole year and it would bring on a panic attack. I was already fearful of almost everything, then I was struggling to go out in public in case it happened in front of people. I had this real fear about fitting and yet I then bought it on myself in later years with alcohol-related seizures.

I think my first alcohol-induced seizure, that I knew of, happened whilst I was in hospital the first time for the drink. I'd been on it big time over Christmas then attempted to stop cold-turkey. As the nurse or doctor was in the room, I had a seizure. I came to with more people around my bed asking me things like my date of birth and who the prime minister was, I had no recollection of what had happened. I always knew when it had happened as I used to pee myself. Even though I got myself into some right states I was never a bed-wetter. Somehow, I always managed to wake when I needed the loo. When a seizure occurred, I could tell as I'd always wee even if I'd not long been to the toilet.

I was known as a frequent flyer at my local hospital and I honestly can't tell you how many times I was admitted, maybe five times, I'm not sure. I was also kicked out of A&E a few times and told to go home and keep drinking which wasn't helpful to Mum as she knew it was on her to start measuring again. Sometimes they would prescribe Valium, along with the advice of weaning me off alcohol. This was a huge responsibility as the Valium had DO NOT DRINK ALCOHOL written all over it.

HOSPITAL

I was in hospital, in a hospital gown and hospital knickers with bare feet. It was nighttime and I decided I was going home. I didn't know where I was or how to get home, but I thought I'd figure that out when I was on the move. I calmly stepped out of bed and walked towards the nurses' station, I thought I'd get out the door near them. On the walk, there were Gollum-like creatures crawling out of cardboard boxes. Were they people or monsters? The boxes were on their sides with the open end facing me. Biggish boxes that came to about my waist. In them were these awful things that were looking at me and crawling out to get me. Shit, they were after me. I didn't know what these things were but I knew they were evil and it was me they were after. They were crawling towards me, snaking out of the boxes. I panicked. There was an old lady with a walking stick and under her chair was a smaller box and an awful creature was coming out of that box and slithering towards me too. I thought I'd get the walking stick and beat them off. It was horrible. I was trapped inside a waking nightmare. There were people around me and I had to fight them off. I needed the walking stick for my weapon. Everyone was closing in on me. I started screaming. Paranoia was getting the better of me and I was so scared. I woke after my horrible dream back in the hospital bed. I'd had a good sleep for once. I'd been pumped to the eyeballs of Librium which was the only thing that seemed to take the edge off the alcohol withdrawal, but highly addictive. I had two drips, one standard and one bright yellow one feeding me B vitamins.

I'd been in hospital for a few nights, and I'd noticed there was always a security guard lurking around. I hadn't paid much attention to this previously but once I started to get my wits about me, not feeling good by any means but a little better, I was curious as to why he was there. The ward was full of elderly ladies so I couldn't work out what his role was. One night I asked him, and he came to sit on the chair next to my bed, looking shocked as to why I didn't know. He told me they had to have someone there for twenty-four hours because of me. Me? I was shocked. Why? He told me I'd ripped down the curtains around my bed and was fighting with the nurses. This is what happened the night the things in boxes were coming to get me. I remember being held down that night by a big nurse and I think they must have jabbed me with something to make me sleep but it was all hazy. It was like a dream that was vivid but when you wake up you can't really remember it. This time it was the other way around, I had been awake but felt like I was dreaming. I ended up chatty with all the security guards and they used to come and sit with me during their shift, they must have been so bored just stood on the ward. The hospital told Mum that I'd been hallucinating and that it can happen during alcohol withdrawal. I certainly was hallucinating, there's no denying that, but I'm not entirely sure it was due to just alcohol. I'm pretty sure the concoction of drugs I'd been fed since being admitted played a part in it too.

There was a lady in the bed next to me who was in her nineties, Gladys. She used to go wandering and the nurses were always getting her back in bed. When I started to feel a little more with it, I'd walk around the ward with her as she was known to take things from people. The nurses would frequently find a stash of glasses where she'd gathered them up from everyone on the ward. Someone would pick up a book to read, reach for their glasses and realise they'd gone missing. Another thing Gladys liked was slippers, she didn't mind whose they were. She'd chatter away and she used to cheer me up. I'd try to help the nurses get on with their work by steering Gladys back towards her bed, even though I was off my nut myself.

I was in hospital again, this time just before Christmas. I can't remember what happened during the lead up to this particular episode. I was in a side room off a men's ward as they had run out of beds. There were only three of us in the room. I was next to Norma, an older lady who was always reading and quoting from the Bible. Opposite Norma was Marlene. The bed opposite me was vacant. I woke up in the room and didn't know how I got there. I'd wet the bed, so I was pretty sure I'd seizured. I asked Norma if she noticed anything, but she told me I'd been asleep. I'd been dreaming I was feeding my cat and dropped something made of glass. It shattered into a million pieces onto the floor tiles and there was glass, shining in every colour, all over the floor. I had to pick the cat up, so he didn't cut his paws or go near his food bowl as there was glass in it. I tried to reach for my cat but there was too much glass and it was too brightly coloured, it was hurting my eyes. My cat started moving, I was panicking. I had to get to him, so he didn't hurt himself. This was another vivid, colourful dream, and I was sure it happened while I was fitting but I'll never know if I did or not, or if I just peed the bed.

Marlene was talking. Talking, talking, talking. In fact, she didn't pause for breath. I was bedbound for a few days, too ill to get up or talk to anyone. Eventually, after the drugs had kicked in and the alcohol had started to wear off, I was able to sit up and talk to Norma. She read to me from the Bible. I was Christened as a child but have never been particularly religious. I now am much more spiritual than I ever was back then as I had to turn inside to try and heal. I was just being polite to Norma and smiling and nodding in all the right places. Why was I being punished so much? I could list a thousand things I'd done that were wrong and I was sorry, I really was. I'd suffered and was still suffering, and I couldn't get out of it. Nothing was fair. It was all my fault. She told me to have belief in God and I again just nodded at her, sick already of hearing Bible quotes. It was shortly after this that prayer came into my life. When you have nothing left and are so low and helpless, prayer is the only thing left on offer. The word prayer can raise a few doubts in some people as it's usually closely followed by the word religion. I personally do not feel that the two are as interconnected as people suspect, or at least needn't be depending on your own personal preference. I had stolen from our local petrol station. They knew me in there and when I was desperate for alcohol and had no money, I'm sorry to say I felt like I had no other option. On the third day in a row, they caught me and said they had CCTV footage. The police were called but the petrol station didn't press charges as I was a regular customer and I had broken down telling them about my dependency. Later that day I wrote a card for them saying how sorry I was, and Mum dropped it in. I was expecting them to tell Mum where to stick it but instead, they said they were all praying for me. They were Muslim and, in that instant, I thought even people with different religions to me, and that I had wronged, were praying for me and wishing me well so it was about time I started praying for myself.

Marlene was talking again, in fact, I think she only stopped when asleep. I tried to blank it all out, the drugs helping with that. As I was getting better, I was starting to hear her, and she was going over the same stuff again and again. Norma used to tell her to shut up and let us sleep, I just tried to do crosswords. I was trying to get my brain back into some kind of functioning form and doing puzzles forced me to think while I was bedbound. On and on the talking, Bible quotes, blood pressure readings, hospital food. It was monotonous. Then it was Christmas eve and Marlene was being discharged although she didn't seem very happy about going. In a weird way I thought I'd miss the chattering as it passed the time. It was just me and Norma left, but shortly after her daughter arrived to take her home for Christmas. Oh well, I thought, it would be me next. Mum came to visit, and we had a row. I don't know what we argued about as I was off my head on medication and alcohol withdrawal. When I was in this much of a mess, I didn't know what I was saying or doing or the reasons why.

Anyone that says the truth outs when you've had a drink doesn't know what they are talking about. I get it that things might slip out after one or two, but when you're dependent and have been drinking non-stop for months on end it certainly isn't the truth that comes out. I have huge regrets in the way I've spoken to Mum, Div, Maca, and many others, but I can't take it back. I can promise I didn't mean half of what I said, I can't even remember saying most of it. Unfortunately, other people always remember, and I can't say sorry enough. During the arguing, I was waiting to go home. The nurse, however, told me I wasn't going home for Christmas. I had a tantrum. Course I was going, I could walk. I got up and paced up and down to prove that I was well enough, I just wanted out of the prison. They said they couldn't as I was still on a high dose of Librium. I told them I was fine. I felt perfectly fine at the time but looking back I was off my nut and most of it was a blur.

Christmas day arrived and I was in the side room alone. The nurses told me to come and sit at the nurses' station with them, where they had boxes of chocolates. They were all happy and getting into the Christmas spirit. I sat talking to the nurses, wishing I was like them. They were looking after the patients with smiles on their faces, no doubt they were worn out but still doing their best to help people. I was miserable and couldn't ever imagine feeling happy again. I was exhausted. I'd probably only sat with them for ten minutes, but it had taken its toll and I was shattered. I went back to bed and actually slept. A peaceful sleep. I was woken later by someone gently tapping my arm. I opened my eyes to see a friendly male nurse. He said I was so sound asleep I missed

Christmas dinner but that he had saved me some. I could've cried had I the energy. One, because I'd slept, and two, because this stranger was being nice to me and I wasn't used to kindness from strangers. I was used to people looking down their nose at me. At this point I'd long given up expecting people to treat me as a human being. It seemed all anyone saw was Alcoholic, not Vanessa, and ignored me when asking questions that should have been for me, directing them straight at Mum. I had given up acting like a human being, with feelings, as it seemed people only talked down at me and told me to stop drinking, no one seemed to care what I was going through as it was classed as self-inflicted. The kind nurse brought me the dinner and I thoroughly enjoyed it. I don't think I'd eaten for ages and the other hospital food hadn't been very nice, but this tasted good. Then I realised I was in a side room on my own, on Christmas day, eating my dinner in a hospital bed, and I was sad. I felt really sorry for myself but feeling sorry didn't outweigh the self-hatred that had already built up inside of me. I was useless. I couldn't even be well. I pissed off everyone around me and I was good for nothing.

Mum had kicked me out a few times when she was at her wit's end during the years this crazy behaviour went on. I just couldn't seem to stop, and she couldn't cope with it. At one point I even ended up calling Maca and going to stay with him on the Isle of Wight. I always called him when things got really tough and it wasn't fair on him, I still regret the way I treated him even now. I was in trouble, so I used him to fall back on for support as I knew he still cared. I was on one of my sessions just before attempting to wean off so was expecting the withdrawal to kick in. He took me back to stay at his house. His family home is pretty big, and I was walking down the stairs after being to the loo. The next thing I knew I was lying on the stairs with Maca on the phone to an ambulance. I told him I was fine and tried to get up, but he forced me back to be seated again. What had happened now? I'd peed all over their new carpet on the stairs. I didn't know how as I'd only just been to the toilet. Maca told me I'd had another seizure. I made it slowly downstairs to his bedroom. I got in bed and was feeling pretty awful. I didn't really understand it. I was now seizuring when I wasn't cutting down on alcohol, so I knew things had got bad. Very bad. Two paramedics turned up. The woman wasn't as understanding or as non-judgmental as the other paramedics I'd encountered. She saw a half-drunk bottle of wine on the bedside table, announced, "Well, you won't be needing that", and took it to the kitchen. Maca was then advised to take me into the garden and give me a good hosing down in freezing water and they left. Helpful. An hour or so later I got a call from the doctor. They must've been notified that the ambulance had been called. I told her what had happened. She asked if I had any drink and I said yes but the paramedic took it off me, but the doctor told me under no circumstances to stop drinking, to have a little in between water. I was already dazed and confused, now the medical staff was confusing me. Which one did I believe? The one that said to carry on drinking of course. I was hating the stuff by this point, but I knew she was right as I'd heard the same words echoed over the past few years. So, I kept on drinking.

SCARED

I'd done it again and was in withdrawal, back home at Mum's. I can't put into words how much I hated myself. All I had left was prayer and hope and I wasn't about to give up either. Mum and Div were just about sticking by me even though I'd put them through hell and I was at it again. This episode was the one following on from the work Christmas masquerade party. I'd been on the booze for about two weeks solid and was trying to come off it. Each withdrawal had got that bit worse which was just unimaginable. Every time I closed my eyes, I saw the Grim Reaper. I used to have to look him in the face/hood and tell him to go away, I wasn't ready. I was so scared. Scared of everything but at this point my main fear was death. The withdrawal was awful. I had Mum back in my room, the bucket was back along with the bedsores. My body kept going numb. I'd lose complete feeling in an arm or leg and when this happened to my legs it made it even more difficult to walk. I was worried I was going to have to have a limb amputated due to alcoholism, something I had read about. I had nothing. I thought I'd hit rock bottom before, but this was really it.

I used to dream of having a husband. One that I totally adored and that loved me back and that we had a nice house and our own family. It was the only thing that kept me going. I still had some inner strength left and I knew it was that tiny iota of strength that was going to get me through. That and pure faith. I had to fight. I was fed up of fighting, most of my life felt like a struggle but I was going to fight it. I was scared shitless of my life being over and what it would do to Mum and Div. I had to get through it and get well. I told Mum I was going to be a glamour model and I think she thought I was off my head. After all, I was a sweating, grey-yellow, puffy mess that couldn't get out of bed. I couldn't even wash. Mum used to have to put me in the bath and scrub me. I was toxic and the smell that was coming out of my pores seemed chemical. My hair had huge chunks of stinking scalp in it amongst the sweat and grease. I think this was from dehydration and generally having an alcohol diet which led to my scalp shedding in big flakes. We'd been here so many times before and were all exhausted.

During the early hours of the 18th December 2012, I had my last alcoholic drink. I believe it was from a cheap box of white wine. I was sleeping in Mum's bed and had managed to go the night with water alone. I was really determined this time. I was so tired and depressed and hated my life, if you could call it that, the way it was. Mum had been feeding me back to health and I'd been eating regularly and been pumped full of healthy food even though I had no appetite and was struggling to keep the food down. I'd had the usual sleep deprivation and I think this night I finally managed a bit of sleep. The next morning, I went to the toilet. Now, this isn't going to be pretty so forgive me for the descriptions but it's part of what happened and what literally scared the shit out of me. I went to the loo and toxic waste fell out. Loads of it. It was the usual unhealthy yellow colour it used to turn during withdrawals. I hadn't been for a few days and was pleased I'd got it out of me as the poison must've been festering in me for a while. I went back to bed with a bit more hope. I was starting to clear out the shit, excuse the pun. Mum was pleased my body was functioning and that I was only drinking water and was feeling hopeful. About an hour later I needed to go again. Again, I can't believe the amount of yellow poo that came out of me. It was kind of normal in texture but was almost luminous in colour. Oh well, I was getting it out that was the main thing. An hour later it happened again. By now I was starting to get a bit worried as I had no idea where all this poo was coming from. It continued, to about every half hour. I swear if it was all piled up in a heap it would amount to the same size as me, I told you this wasn't going to be a pretty story. I was exhausted. All this pooing on the half hour had literally taken it out of me and I was doubly worried about dehydration. I continued with the water and the poo kept coming. It then turned to pure liquid and it was like pouring a whole bucket of yellow slimy water down the loo. By now I was feeling really rough. I just needed sleep. I tried to sleep but there was a gurgling in my stomach and another bucketful of luminous yellow water escaped me. I went back to bed holding onto the walls for support. It happened again. This time it had really done me. I walked towards Mum's room, but it looked like I was walking down an invisible staircase. Each step I took I got closer and closer to the floor. I was laid out on the floor and Mum got on the phone to call an ambulance. She could see how pale I was, and she later admitted she thought she had lost me there and then. I couldn't even talk, there was nothing left in me. I was so gutted. Earlier that day I'd started to believe I could do it and was so determined. However, physically all I could do was lay on the floor and pray. The ambulance arrived and I was carted back to hospital.

I was in a side room again, this time alone. As I'd had such a bad tummy, they couldn't put me on a ward until they had ruled out that it wasn't a contagious bug. When I was seen I experienced one of the nicer consultants. She was caring but she put the fear of God in me. She told me I needed the usual blood tests, I was used to those, and I told her I was worried about my liver due to all the yellow that had been coming out of me. She listed all the other damage I could have done to my organs. I was having tests but if it was bad, I was worried I might not be able to go to the toilet on my own again. I was also worried that I would lose the use of my arms or legs due to the continual numbness. I was in total despair. I hated myself but I clung onto hope, the only thing I had left. She was so kind and when she talked to Mum, she explained her son was also an alcoholic and she was powerless over it. She was nice because she understood it more than most as she was also going through it.

The tests, thank God, were OK. I was put on the usual drips and left on my own in the side room. At first, I couldn't make it to the toilet even though there was one in my room, so I had to buzz for a nurse to bring me a bedpan. When my strength started to build, I was able to make it to the loo but only with assistance as I couldn't manage the short walk on my own. I was drinking loads of water. They needed me to do a poo sample but after the amount that had come out of me previously, I never thought I'd need to go again! I was having to eat, eat and eat some more so they could do the tests. It turned into a joke when the nurses asked me what I wanted for my meals as they'd give me everything from the menu anyway. Finally, I managed to go, and no virus or bug was found. As I suspected it was just alcohol that was the culprit. If I wasn't sleeping, I was out of my bed trying to move about and get my circulation going. I was still suffering from tingling and numb limbs and it was really worrying. When I wasn't trying to move about in the few square feet of space I had, I was trying to use my brain doing puzzles from a magazine. The radiators were pumping out stuffy heat and I was in my underwear most of the time, sweating. The big old windows opened about two inches at the bottom and I used to get up as close as I could to feel fresh air on my face and try to feel alive.

During this hospital visit, two people came to my room from the outreach centre offering help. I'd already tried help and it had failed me. Something shifted within me and I was feeling calm and a little voice in the back of my head told me I had nothing left to lose, so I agreed.

HELP

I didn't find help and support for my alcoholism easily, contrary to the belief that once you admit it is a problem you are on the road to recovery. Yes, it's a start but then it was a very long road for me. It's a taboo subject and some of the advice I was given was utter shit. Over the years I was looked down at, talked down to, sneered at, lectured and ignored. What no one seemed to remember was that I was still a human being, already feeling isolated and alone. I was in and out of doctors' surgeries for years but there wasn't much they could do apart from refer me to the local addiction centre, advise me to stop drinking, or offer antidepressants. I never saw the point of taking medication as I knew it was alcohol causing me the issues I had. Yes, I felt depressed at times but that was because alcohol is a depressant. I couldn't continue to drink and take antidepressants, it just seemed a counterproductive idea to me, besides I think my liver had enough of a job to process all the alcohol let alone medication too. I was also told on quite a few occasions that I didn't look like an alcoholic which didn't help me in the slightest. I was seeing GPs to try and get help with my problem, but some seemed to question whether I really was an alcoholic as I apparently didn't look like one. I was telling them I was sleeping with vodka under the pillow, yet they looked like they disbelieved me as I didn't look how they expected. This amazed me as it shouldn't have mattered what I looked like, or even how much I was drinking. I was telling them it had become a problem for me, yet I wasn't always taken seriously. Another thing I often got told was that I was too young to be an alcoholic. I'm not sure how alcoholism is professionally diagnosed but as I mentioned previously if it has become a problem for someone then it is already a problem for them, regardless of the scale.

Over the years I had gone to the local addiction centre for help. The main problem with the place, and there were many, was that as soon as you'd been a week or so without alcohol you were discharged, and they gained a statistic of curing someone. They had a great reputation and were known as one of the best in the borough, statistically, but the people who had been 'treated' there knew different. I was asked the usual question; how much do I drink? *How long is a piece of string?* When I was in utter despair, desperation, and depression it escaped my mind to start working out units and tallying them up. Some days I wouldn't drink but they needed answers for their tick-box sheet. I told them what an extreme day was like and what a good day was like when I had nothing. I don't know how they marked this on my records. They gave me a little plastic cup which shows the unit measurements on the side. Great, I could drink out of a plastic cup now instead of straight from the bottle. That made its way to our bathroom in which it served as a toothbrush holder for a while. Once I was given great advice from one of the textbook-taught workers there. She suggested I got a boyfriend. I wasn't going out at this point, didn't have many friends left, was unemployed and had no money. I asked her how I went about this and she suggested going to the cinema. I asked if she thought it was a good idea for me to go to the cinema alone and stumble around in the dark trying to find a man, to which she had no answer to. I was in and out of this place for years and all it did was frustrate me, it wasn't in the least bit helpful. To paint the picture, the staff at the reception desk used to be behind one of those protective glass screens. There was security on the door and the chairs were nailed to the floor. There were people banging on the door for methadone, they didn't mind dishing that out like Smarties even though no one wants to be on the stuff but hey ho, they replace heroin with methadone and gain yet another statistic of 'curing' someone. There were people with cans of Special Brew in the waiting area and no one wanted to be there.

My file ended up being about a foot tall with all the paperwork. I'd been 'cured' by them so many times on paper. In reality, I'd just finished the current binge and was going well for a while before things got dark again. One good thing did come out of this place. I was allocated a counsellor, Trevor. Having had the previous experience, I wasn't really looking forward to meeting him, but I did, and he told me he was a recovering alcoholic. OK, this was someone I might listen to. He showed me the chip he had from AA marking his seventeen years of sobriety. At the time I scoffed at him that I didn't want to be collecting chips from AA, thank you very much, and he asked why. I'd always turned my nose up at it. I guess I didn't want to stop completely, I just wanted to go back to being a social drinker, something that didn't happen anymore. I wanted to go back to when alcohol was fun and not a career, but even when I had a 'normal' drink it never ended up being normal. I knew the only thing was abstinence, but I wasn't ready then. So in between meeting with Trevor, the others at the centre gave me advice on how to be a 'regular drinker'. Looking back this is just so sodding ridiculous I don't know what to say. When you've passed the invisible line into alcoholism there is no going back to social drinking. Alcoholism is progressive, there is no going back. Normal drinking for addicts is never normal and yet here was a whole centre dedicated to helping people return to *that*, even though *that* didn't exist. It was like they were just telling alcoholics what they wanted to hear. However, their stats were great so, clearly, they all knew what they were talking about. What a joke.

I would listen to Trevor and I liked him. I must've been a pain in the arse to him because I still had a certain arrogance and determination about me, he must've felt he was talking to a brick wall. Counselling is a strange thing. You can sit and go through your darkest moments and pour your heart out. The counsellor can offer suggestions or keep you talking to get it out and you don't always give it much thought at the time. I used to leave there feeling a little more positive with a few of his sayings going around in my head but then it was forgotten. However sometimes, even years later, a little snippet of what was discussed can pop into my head and make perfect sense. I guess it just happens at the right time and place for that individual. I still remember a few of the things Trevor said to me and at the time I just dismissed. One thing he mentioned was for me to never lose my sense of humour. I'd see him in some real states, but I'd always find something to laugh about. Another was that I should write a book.

Trevor thought it was best for me to go into rehab. I'd said, "No, no, no" on many occasions. I realised I had nothing else and wasn't working so would give it a go, although I was just going through the motions. I didn't want to and my heart wasn't in it. Over time, I'd talked myself round and finally had accepted going. He said I was top of the waiting list and it shouldn't be a long wait. I got myself psyched up for it, accepted it, and then almost looked forward to trying it. I then went to see someone else, I can't remember why, for some kind of paper tick-box exercise, and when I mentioned rehab, they looked at me blankly. They said I wasn't going, and I wasn't on the list. It wasn't in my file. My file would've taken an avid reader about a year to get through, so I asked again but was faced with nothing. I left and told Mum who was waiting in the reception area which caused a row. I know the common belief of alcoholics and addicts being liars, cheats, and thieves, but I wasn't lying. She didn't believe me and thought I'd just said that to get out of rehab, but I didn't. I was top of the list and then there was no list. I told Trevor the next time I saw him, and he looked defeated and was very apologetic. I knew it wasn't his fault, it was the system. All in all, I think he must've thought we got nowhere during our little meetings but the fact I still remember him fondly now means he did play a part in my recovery, albeit years later.

During one of my sessions with Trevor, he told me he couldn't do my counselling anymore. He didn't really have answers, it was all due to 'the system'. I could tell he was beaten and disappointed, although his meetings with me couldn't have felt very productive for him. He couldn't explain why but they were changing things and he would no longer be allocated to me, but I'd have someone new. The new counsellor thought he was a joker but wasn't funny. One of those that when you ask if they are alright reply, "No, I'm half left", or tell me, "It's nice weather for ducks" when it was raining. Hilarious. When I started talking to him about my drinking, he told me he'd never touched the stuff as he was a strict Muslim. Well, why the fuck was he counselling me through alcohol abuse then?! I gave him one more try as I don't believe in giving up (look how long it took me to give up the drink). I realised I was right the first time, he was a total cock-head and I couldn't take advice from him. Besides he had none to offer. I was always advised to, "Just stop drinking" by all. No shit, Sherlock.

During my hospital visits, I received a mixture of concern and a complete lack of it. Some of the doctors and nurses were genuinely really caring and others weren't. I heard that during medical training only half a day is spent training on addiction. I'm not sure how true this is but, in my experience, it seems like it could be the case. Hospitals are filled with alcohol and addiction related illnesses and accidents, yet no one seems to want to give it much focus.

Once when I'd been admitted a nurse turned to my mum and stated, "My son is her age and he doesn't do that to himself".

Well done her, one-nil. A doctor I saw in A&E once sounded like he was auditioning for a role on Casualty. He made sure he spoke at the top of his voice so all could hear how busy he was and what a waste of time I was to him. He kept asking me if I was passing blood from my back passage to which I kept replying no. He didn't want me staying in, another dirty alcoholic taking up a hospital bed, so told me unless I wanted him to check for bleeding by him inserting a finger then I was to leave. He said it to humiliate me. He then proceeded to knead my tummy like I was some kind of stiff dough he was working up into a loaf of bread, purposely trying to make me feel uncomfortable. Mum witnessed this and saw how I was treated. He sent me on my not-so-merry way saying to self-medicate with alcohol and come off gradually. Oh, and then to stop drinking.

Another time, whilst in overnight, the doctor appeared with a look of disgust. Yes, I was a dirty alcoholic and I knew all about it. He told me to go home and that I was discharged. I was attempting to get up out of bed although in comparison this was like me attempting to climb Everest, when one of the nurses stopped me and asked me what I was doing. I told her the doctor had discharged me. She looked at my notes and said under no circumstances was I discharged. My notes stated what medication I was to be on throughout the night and they weren't letting me go. The next morning the same doctor came to sneer down his nose at me. He said, "You decided to stay then, this isn't a hotel". I told him the nurses wouldn't allow me to leave but no one believes an alcoholic and he just left giving me a filthy look. I thought doctors were meant to be non-judgemental?

One morning when asked if I could manage breakfast I opted for porridge. I hadn't eaten in days and was finally getting a bit of an appetite. As I was about to take my second much-needed mouthful, a nurse rushed over and grabbed the spoon from my mouth and took the bowl away with a filthy look. She asked me what the hell I thought I was doing. Erm, attempting to eat something, I hadn't eaten in ages. She said I was nil-by-mouth and should know better. I wasn't aware of this as no one had actually told me and it wasn't written on the board above my bed. The look of utter disgust on her face said it all. It wasn't worth arguing that no one had told me because she never would have believed me, I was just a lying alcoholic. I was due to go for an endoscopy as there had been blood in my vomit, but no one told me this or I would have politely refused the porridge.

THE CENTRE

As promised, the outreach team that visited me in hospital contacted me a few days after arriving home after being discharged from hospital. I'd forgotten about meeting them and didn't think they'd follow up on it. I had no faith in the system due to the way I was treated at the last place. I was still too ill to leave the house, so they kept calling me back every few days. These guys just weren't giving up, but I had. I started ignoring calls and isolating. I was still feeling weak, ill and helpless. After a while, I answered one of their calls to get them off my back and I ended up agreeing to go with them to a local place which I will refer to as The Centre. I'd heard of it and knew it was a day rehab, people I'd met through AA had spoken very highly about it and recommended it. I had visions in my mind of everyone being confined in beds for the day on a ward doing some colouring in or painting, letting out their 'feelings'. I could imagine people walking around drugged up to the eyeballs, screaming, or just sitting in a corner rocking back and forth. I guess I still wanted to be that 'normal' drinker and go back to drinking on occasions, so I didn't want to hear of places that had helped 'cure' people. I was scared to give up entirely and couldn't get my head around life without alcohol, no crutch to lean on, even though the other part of me desperately wanted to rid it from my life. Although people meant well, I was getting frustrated with people telling me they knew how I felt when they had absolutely no idea. I once had a discussion with a GP about this who told me that you don't have to have a heart attack to know how one feels, but we had to agree to disagree on that one. How can someone possibly know what you are going through if they haven't been through it, or something similar, themselves? It's just things people say to try and ease the pain and although I appreciate that, it didn't help. I remember once just after Dad died someone telling Mum they knew exactly what she was going through as they had recently lost their dog! I know only too well the heartache of losing a beloved pet, but this was no comparison. People seemed to always be telling me they understood me and how I felt when they really couldn't even comprehend.

Then the day arrived, and the outreach guys were on the doorstep. I recognised one as one of the two that had visited me in hospital. I got in the car and went with them. I arrived and The Centre wasn't at all what I imagined. It looked cosy and like a normal little house. I went and sat on a comfy sofa with one of the ladies that worked there. We went through the standard form and I was asked how much I drank on an average day. That dreaded fucking question yet again. I think I flipped a bit, but she completely understood. I then learnt that the people that ran the place were recovering alcoholics that had trained to become counsellors. OK, now they had my attention.

I was registered onto the day program. This involved being abstinent from alcohol and drugs, attending The Centre daily for two weeks. I didn't have anything else going on and was starting to feel a bit more human, though still really not right in the head. I had time, so much time. My days used to fly by in a drunken stupor but now I wasn't drinking everything was dragging and I didn't know what to do with myself. What did I do with all the time? What did 'normal' people do? I didn't know who I was and wasn't even sure of my likes or dislikes. I had no hobbies so most of the days were just me passing time, mostly living in my head, with not much to do. I needed to top up on something but couldn't use alcohol and had no idea how else to top up, or even what I was trying to top up. Something was missing in me. I was starting to get feelings back - shock horror - drink numbs those bad boys, but I didn't know what to do with the feelings. I wasn't even sure how to really feel. I was still numb. I felt better physically but mentally I was all over the place.

I arrived on my first day and was taken down to the kitchen area. There was already someone in the kitchen who greeted me and shook my hand. He was very smartly dressed in a suit and I assumed he worked there. It turned out he was on the day program too and made me feel very welcome. I felt like a stranger but somehow knew this was where I needed to be. Gradually people started to arrive, and teas and coffees were made. All who entered the kitchen said hello to me and introduced themselves. I couldn't believe how friendly everyone was. All were in a different stage of recovery, some fresh like me, and some that had been coming for months. The main trend seemed to be a lot of biscuit eating. As alcohol is loaded with sugars, eating sweet food in early recovery relieved some of the cravings.

We were called into the first group. I had no idea what to expect but decided fear couldn't get the better of me this time and I just had to do what was required of me. It was a smallish group of people, maybe ten, and we were sat on chairs in a circle. The first session of the day was meditation. I'd never attempted meditation before and didn't really realise what it involved but thought why not? The lights were dimmed, and a guided meditation reading was put on. We all just had to close our eyes, relax and listen. I closed my eyes but felt a total dick and wondered if they were having me on. I sneaked one eye open to look around at the group, but they were all getting involved so I took their lead and attempted it myself. It helped to calm me. I was a little shocked as I didn't imagine starting the day off like this but then again, I had no idea what to expect. When it finished, I did feel a bit lighter, I guess. I quite enjoyed it. It wasn't a session you had to attend, and a few opted out but that was usually due to anxiety.

More people had turned up whilst we were meditating and there must've been 15-20 people in the next session. A male counsellor led the group and I took an instant like to him. He was a recovering alcoholic and just seemed to get things. We were sat in a circle and he started on his left asking each of us to explain how our weekend had been. I thought I'd better listen, and I did. There were mixed answers. Some had a good time and were pleased with themselves for staying clean from drink or drugs, others were struggling. One guy had a panic attack and I could see he really tried to talk through it, but it got the better of him and he had to leave. My heart was already pounding as it was nearing my turn to talk but knowing that everyone there seemed so sympathetic and understanding, and that other people appeared to be struggling more than I was, eased my nerves slightly although that sounds a bit mean. Also, they all had their own problems to worry about. It got to my turn, so I used this as an opportunity to introduce myself and let people know how bad my drinking had got. I couldn't have spoken for more than five minutes but the fact was I did it, and in front of a room full of people all looking at me. I think once it was past my turn, I tended to zone out a bit and not give the others my full attention as I was shocked and relieved of what I'd just managed to do. This was huge for me. Not only was I with a group of strangers and publicly talking I'd also poured my heart out and it didn't kill me. Actually, there was a sense of freedom lurking and although still not feeling right I was very pleased with myself.

In between sessions which lasted about an hour, we had breaks where we went to the kitchen or the smokers went outside. I'd always been a bit of an occasional smoker but at this point I wasn't smoking at all. I stayed in the kitchen and had coffee and no doubt a few biscuits. The counsellors always said that the best therapy happened during the breaks and I understand this now. We were just human beings with a common problem. We'd sit and talk, and I couldn't believe the things we were telling each other as practically strangers. Once anyone started it all came pouring out, we were all kind of fighting for the spotlight and there was a lot of talking. I really liked these people, I liked them all. I felt a strong sense of connection. I'd always kind of felt like the odd one out no matter who I was with, and at last I had a sense of belonging. There was always plenty of laughter, after all if we weren't laughing, we'd be crying. Break time over and we went for the next session. It all finished just after lunchtime.

At the end of each day, we were all set tasks. Someone had to arrange the rota and then find people for duties for the week which included washing up, hoovering and cleaning the toilets. It was all kept nice and tidy and I noticed people had even volunteered for the loo cleaning. I did all the duties and the loo cleaning wasn't bad at all as everyone looked after the place. I just wanted to feel like I was helping. When I left for the day it was an odd feeling. Something had lightened in me, but my head was whirling with all the information I'd taken in, and all the things other people had said about their addiction. I couldn't believe there were other people out there that did similar things to me. Really horrendous, damaging things, but we could open up to each other. I definitely felt better leaving than I did going in, but I couldn't put my finger on what I was actually feeling. The thoughts continued swirling through my mind for the afternoon, but I just went along with it without trying to reason or question anything. My routine back then used to be to get home and exercise. I had about thirty exercise DVDs so as soon as I got home, I'd do one. I seemed to have loads of newfound energy that I needed to use as it was building inside of me. During one of the sessions, we were asked to describe ourselves as a metaphor. I answered that I was a Duracell bunny. I had so much energy, but I didn't know what to do with it. I slept well after the days I was at The Centre as I'd been so busy concentrating and listening then churning all the things over in my head which left me mentally exhausted.

I went back and I completed my two weeks. I still loved the morning guided meditations. We also did a women only group once a week which was a laugh in the scheme of things, even though what we were talking about was no laughing matter. I'd never had much female company and they were a nice group. The groups would change from week to week where people would leave and new people would start, but there was always a sense of belonging. Once a week they used to have someone come in to do a chair. I really looked forward to this session as it was an ex-addict of some description that had got themselves dry or clean or both and came in to tell us of their experience. They all had a varying number of years of recovery and were ex-group members from The Centre. They all mentioned how the place had saved their lives and I was beginning to understand what they meant.

My two weeks were up but I wasn't ready to leave. I wasn't expecting this considering I was reluctant to go in the first place. During the time I was there, you could stay on for longer if needed. I ended up staying about ten weeks, I felt I couldn't leave. It was so comfortable and yet what we talked about was uncomfortable. It opened you up and left you raw but then the healing started. The people were what made it, it was an eye-opener and very therapeutic. I'd mentioned during the groups my urgency to get back to work and earn money. I was still at Mum's and not giving her a penny, I literally didn't have any pennies, and was feeling guilty. I also knew I had to get back into it before fear got the better of me. During the earlier weeks of my visits, everyone voiced their concerns about me giving myself more time before I went back to work, which I didn't want to hear. Now I know why they said it, I wasn't ready earlier on in my recovery. In the grand scheme of things, I'd been drinking constantly for about a decade so a few extra weeks off to take care of myself and get well wouldn't matter but in the back of my mind there was a sense of urgency to get back on track. I'd been doing the odd photo shoot at weekends as was looking much fresher and still had this energy and sense of lost-time. I was going for it full on. Probably a bit too much but it didn't do me any harm. I'd spent years in my pit drinking in the dark and then feeling so ill or being hospitalised that I was making the most of my time, which now felt free. At weekends sometimes The Centre offered additional day programs. One I attended was a Step 1 group. The first step, based on the 12 Steps of AA, is *We admitted we were powerless over alcohol - that our lives had become unmanageable.* 'We' being the operative word, you cannot do this recovery thing alone. We sat as a group and were each handed a notepad and asked to write down all the awful things that we had done in our addiction. I started writing, and writing, and writing. I nearly filled the notepad. We then got together in smaller groups and spoke about the things we'd written. At first, it was a little awkward as I didn't really know the other two in my group. Then we opened our souls up for others to see. Once we started, we were all fighting to say our bit. We started to realise that we'd all done horrifically bad things and we had to get it all out in the open. There was plenty of laughter. We had to laugh about some of the ridiculous situations we had been in and there were a few hugs when things got teary. It was a real cleanser. It was so nice to share with people who understood and had similar experiences as I'd honestly thought it was just me that did some of the awful things I had. I recently re-read that notepad and had forgotten how shocking it was. I would share it here but it's far too bad to broadcast, so I'll keep that for my own memory as it's important to remember how bad things got. I couldn't possibly have listed all the things that had happened during my alcoholism as the list seemed endless, I feel some of it is too bad and shameful to put down in writing.

Eventually I got a job. I'd spent ten weeks at The Centre and felt ready. I was gutted to be leaving, I could've stayed there forever with the pull that it had but I knew it was time to move on. I don't think I got upset on my last day, although I did feel a loss. I was looking forward to the future for once and although I'd really miss the place and the people, I felt it was time. I was always advised to continue with recovery as the further you get away from recovery the closer you get to relapse. I think I only attended one AA session during the time I was at The Centre, some people were going almost daily as soon as they left the day program. I then found out that The Centre had an aftercare group that ran one evening a week. I put my name down straight away, I was to return the following week for my weekly group sessions. There was no way I wanted to attempt things on my own again. I'd tried for what seemed like a million times and it never worked, no matter how much effort I put in, so this time, I thought I'd stick with others.

EX MEN

Whilst I was attending the day programme at The Centre, I was single which was another first for me. I'd always had boyfriends since a teenager but after my last bender, I'd decided enough was enough. Previously I didn't feel right being single, it was like I always had to be with someone to feel whole as just me wasn't enough. I was trying to fill the hole in the soul. Most of the time I didn't seem to care who I was with, just so long as there was someone. Over the years I'd had my fair share of crap boyfriends. I'm not for one minute saying I was a great girlfriend as I was on and off with the drinking, but I paid the price for it. Over the years and by different people I was controlled. I think some of them liked to think they could be the one that 'cured' me by being a have a go hero, but they really hated being with me. They wanted to be the rescuer but didn't rescue me, in fact, most of them made me feel much worse. I was absolutely no angel, but I also don't believe I deserved some of the treatment I received from some of these exes. One of them held a gun to my head as I was sleeping, the cold feeling of the metal woke me. I looked into the mirrored wardrobes adjacent to the bed and I could see him sitting behind me with a gun and a smirk on his face. Panic isn't a word I can use to appropriately explain the fear that took over me. Time froze and after what felt like hours, he fell about laughing. Apparently, it was a replica and he thought it would be funny to see my reaction. Yes, that was hilarious. I never fancied him in the first place. I actually really disliked him from the moment I met him yet ended up with him for years which proved I couldn't be alone. It was almost like I had to have the attention from someone because I didn't like myself enough, and even bad attention was better than none.

I was pulled downstairs by my ankles, bitten and spat at by another. This one used to have bouts of serious anger which I just antagonised in my drunken stupors. When I called the police about this one individual following being on the receiving end of one of his rages, I was the one removed from the flat. The police really weren't bothered about a domestic even though I was bruised, they just seemed to roll their eyes and make sure they removed the alky. I had the pleasure of paying a hefty bill to spend the night in a hotel that the police escorted me to. I was the one that called them for help, yet I was being treated the criminal. I couldn't afford the cost but had no choice but to pay, leaving me with no money. I had no alcohol to see me through the night or the next morning which could've been fatal in the dependent state I was in.

Another boyfriend completely controlled me while he was out with anyone he could get with behind my back. After four years of being with him, again someone I really didn't fancy in the first place and who repulsed me, the control got worse. We were living together, and he used to disable my car so I couldn't get anywhere alone. I have no idea about cars so I'm not sure what he did or how he did it, but I'd put the keys into the ignition, and nothing would happen. This meant that if I needed to go anywhere, such as work, he would take me. And meet me for lunch. And take me home. My work colleagues thought it was sweet that he used to do that for me, but they didn't realise it was because he wouldn't let me out of his sight. One night I'd really had enough. I'd been trying to break up with him for weeks on end, but he kept threatening suicide. In the end, I seemed left with no option but to up and leave as I knew it was just words to keep me where he wanted me. He'd hidden any phones in the house, so I went to leg it out the door, but he caught me first and physically dragged me back into the house. I tried again later to get out the back door, but he grabbed me and slammed me into the downstairs bathroom with such force I took tiles off the side of the bath when I came into contact with them with my face. I erupted and grabbed an empty glass bottle from the table which was being used as a vase for some flowers he had bought me, attempting to get into my good books. I'd been drinking, no surprises there, and I was at my wits end so to make a point I threw the bottle at his head. What I wanted to do was scare him, so he knew I meant business and to let me out of the house he was keeping me prisoner in. I aimed for just next to his head and my shot was perfect. It smashed on the kitchen cupboard just by his head and did give him a shock. There was glass, water and flowers everywhere, yet he still wrestled with me to keep me in the house which lead to a few cuts and bruises from the broken bottle when he was dragging me to the floor. I gave in and told him I was going to bed. As soon as he thought I was settled, I started to climb out of the bedroom window in pure desperation and was willing to jump to get away from him and risk any injuries. Anything was better than being locked up with him. He caught me in the act and pulled me back into the prison. After weeks and weeks of this behaviour, I eventually managed to rid him from my life, but it was far from easy.

Another used to say he'd stick by me no matter what. However, if I went on the drink, he'd drop me back on Mum's doorstep. He'd call a week or so after to see how I was and if I was still bad, I didn't hear from him until I'd fully recovered, then he'd take me back. Hardly for better or for worse. Most of my exes seemed to do alright out of me for money. I used to pay my way, way too much actually, and a lot of them took advantage of my generous nature. I really had had it with the men in my life. Apart from Maca, most of them hadn't exactly treated me well. Also, they seemed to think they could get away with it as no one believes an alcoholic. A valuable lesson learnt by me was not to go out with someone just for the sake of it again. When I started attending The Centre, I made a pact to myself - no more. I decided if I ever was to be with anyone again, I'd have to fancy them from the start. I think fancying is seriously underrated and if it's not there from the off it doesn't appear later on down the line, no matter how much I had willed it to in the past. If there was ever anyone again it'd have to be for real. When I found recovery, I was happy to just be me, a new me, and be alone. If I didn't find anyone then I'd accepted that. I couldn't carry on the way I had been anymore.

BACK TO WORK

I mentioned I only left The Centre as I got a job. The interview was quite informal, so I wasn't sure how it went. I was worried about all the gaps on my CV and didn't fancy trying to explain it was because I didn't know where I was or what I was doing due to alcoholism, but luckily that wasn't mentioned as the interviewer was more interested in my previous experience. It was a contract role back on an IT service desk and later that week I got a call from my agent being offered the job. I was thrilled.

I soon got into the swing of things and was back on the phones, a job I knew well. I loved being busy again. This is when I met Wayne. I knew from the off that he was my cup of tea and I admit I fancied him at first sight. The problem was he was my manager. Also, I found out he was with someone and had three children. I had to push any hope to the back of my mind and over time we became good friends. Somewhere along the line Wayne and his partner split up, they hadn't had a proper relationship for years and were gradually slipping apart. It was very difficult for him as he didn't want to leave the children but knew it was the right thing to do. I was doing the modelling at weekends, I had this new confidence bubbling away in me somewhere and I felt so good compared to where I had come from. I'd been the lowest of the low, my rock bottom, and when I compared my life to what it was previously, I just felt brilliant in comparison. I truly was grateful for my recovery and never underestimated where the drink took me.

In my second week of work, everyone went to the pub before the long Easter weekend. I'd not been in a pub or anywhere wet since being in recovery, so it felt a little weird. I decided from the off that the safest thing for me to do was be honest with people. When I said I'd come but I don't drink I got the usual, "You can have one", "Party pooper" type comments so I told them I had a drinking problem. These were new work colleagues, including the team leaders and Wayne, the boss, and yet they accepted me saying that. Instead of people being funny with me about it, which was what I expected, they genuinely wanted to know more and how it became an issue. It's very difficult to explain this as people expect the usual, that something happened to me to turn me into an alcoholic. But I was just an alcoholic, it was that simple. I now don't believe it matters what made it happen or how it happens to some and not others, it just does. Finding out what caused it may help if something did actually cause it and counselling is needed, but there isn't always something that starts it. It just happened with me, it's a progressive illness and it will confuse me even more trying to analyse the reason why rather than just accepting that it became a huge problem for me. For years doctors and counsellors, excluding those at The Centre, had pressed me to find out what made me an alcoholic and what triggered it and I drove myself insane trying to work it out. Nothing particularly happened, there was no trigger point. It gradually just got worse as it's a chronic illness. No one sets out with the intention of becoming an alcoholic and it doesn't happen overnight. I'd driven myself mad in the past as so many people asked what caused it that I began to believe something terrible must have happened to me when I was young and that I had blocked it out. I'd go over and over it in my head but never got the answer because there wasn't one. If someone had cancer and found out what caused it, it doesn't cure their cancer. It's the treatment everyone needs to focus on and that was where my focus was channelled, not looking for reasons why. I don't blame people for asking, they are just ignorant to the touchy subject and genuinely think something happens in your life and overnight you become an alcoholic. For me, and many others, it was gradual. The problem is no one, including some of the medical profession, believe this. Many people tried to pin it down to me losing my dad, but I knew it wasn't that and that my drinking was not right before that happened.

I went to the pub with my new team members and again felt like it was another first for me. I'd been totally honest with my work colleagues that I had a drinking problem, and no one turned their back on me. They still all talked to me and I was still part of the team. Another first was that I went out in only my second week with people I didn't know. I've always been so shy, but I guess The Centre and modelling brought out some inner confidence and self-belief for which I will be eternally grateful. Work went well and after six months I applied for a permanent position and was successful. I was grateful for the opportunity, I hadn't had a permanent role for thirteen years. The paperwork started to go through. During this time Wayne and I remained close friends. We'd go out to lunch together and take our cigarette breaks together. At this point, I'd started smoking again. I felt I needed something to be a bit naughty and a few occasionally turned into about fifteen a day but I was still in early recovery and felt that was the least of my worries, I'd deal with that at a later date. As part of the application, I had to complete the occupational health form where there was a question about whether I'd ever been addicted to alcohol or drugs. I spoke to my team leader and Wayne before answering this as I didn't want to get myself in any trouble but in the end, we decided that honesty was the best policy, so I ticked yes. Well, that was a mistake. A few weeks later I got a letter through to go and see one of the internal occupational health doctors. I went along and all she kept saying was if I was to drink again, they would support me. I told her I had no intention of drinking again and I was taking it one day at a time. Looking back, I don't believe she knew anything about recovery. She was basically giving me the green light to drink. If I did, and oh I did want to at times, she told me I wouldn't lose my job over it, I'd just need to contact them. It had planted the seed that drinking was OK, and I could feel the rage building inside me. I told her they were viewing it wrong and that could be a dangerous thing to say to someone in early recovery. She clearly just didn't get it, that half a day training on addiction medical staff got just wasn't enough. I then had to get a letter from The Centre to prove that I was still attending aftercare and I was sent for blood tests, basically to prove my innocence. I was made to feel like a criminal again. My self-worth felt destroyed and I felt judged, yet again having to try and explain myself. I had already been offered the job, that meant that they believed I was well in the mind to be able to cope, and I'd already proved myself for six months, but they wanted more; they literally wanted blood. I was fuming and the doctor knew it. I didn't raise my voice, but I was clearly upset and annoyed. As she was writing my notes, she was doing it with a very shaky hand. I went back to the office and straight to Wayne. Upset had taken over and I felt so rubbish having to prove myself all over again, I was sick of the fighting. Wayne spoke to his boss and they both went down to Occupational Health together. I was told I didn't have to go for a blood test, but it would go down as refused which would look worse, so I ended up agreeing. A few weeks later I reluctantly had my blood taken. Then I heard nothing. Nothing at all, not even an acknowledgement. I emailed the doctor directly and asked if there was a problem. I got a waffly email back about how my blood was lost being sent to the hospital. We were working for the same fucking hospital it was sent to! All of that for nothing. The doctor didn't have the bottle to ask me to re-take it and agreed I would no longer need to be seen. I was still upset, it just wasn't the right way to go about a delicate situation by telling me, "It was OK to drink", just so long as I called in and let them know so they could support me. My mind then went into overdrive. At least the tests had been lost and not mixed up. I hadn't lied, I hadn't drunk for nine months but it would have been awful if it had got mixed up and someone else's had come back. Another six months later a team leader role became available. I'd only been there a year and been sober for a year and three months. There were quite a few people on the desk who were interested in the role that had been there longer than me, so I wasn't sure if I should go for it. I plucked up the courage to apply and couldn't believe it when I was successful. I'm sure there was the odd comment about Wayne getting me the job. Everyone always saw us together, we were pretty much work-wife and work-husband by then and always went on breaks together, but he didn't want anything to do with the decision because of what people might think. In only a year I'd gone from contract to perm and had then worked my way to team leader. I was really pleased with myself considering where I had been the previous year.

Eventually, after Wayne had been split from his ex for a while we got together, yes you guessed it. When we first got together, he was a broken man. He was constantly beating himself up about leaving the kids and thought it would do them some permanent damage not having their dad around, even though they saw him two or three times a week. At first it was really difficult. It seemed like it was never going to settle but over time it calmed down and the kids accepted it.

We've been together for a while now and we've recently bought our first house which we are settled in, and both love. I do believe in fate and that our paths were meant to cross. If I hadn't have got sacked from my previous job then I would never have applied for this one and met Wayne, so I believe that things do happen for a reason. Wayne and I recently got engaged, this time for real! I met the kids years ago and now I'm accepted as part of their life. At the beginning, they got to know me gradually and I never forced myself upon them, I just let them come to me in their own time. In no time, his twin girls got quite attached to me and when they were about five years old, I couldn't go anywhere without one each side of me or sitting on my lap, they wouldn't leave my side. Now I'm just part of the furniture to them.

The battle I have now is trying to get life insurance. I've been sober for over six years but because it's on my doctors' notes I'm screwed. The first quote I looked into getting I was outright refused. I called to ask why, and it was because I had been previously referred to a drug or alcohol centre. I was left fuming again. They didn't even whack the cost up just outright refused me. It seems like if you don't get help and it's not on your paperwork then it's fine, you will get insurance with no problem. However, if like me, you admitted you needed help and did the right thing then you get screwed over. Some of the insurance companies don't even have a date as to how long ago you received help, it stays on there for life. It feels like no matter how long I have been sober for there are still hurdles and people don't allow you move on from your past. It infuriates me that people who have received help are penalised for it. They got help because they recognised they needed it and wanted to put a stop to the problem.

STILL RECOVERING

I am still wholeheartedly grateful for my recovery. Back when I started work and had just left The Centre, I continued with the aftercare group and still do. Although I've moved from the area, I get to spend the night I'm at the group at my mum's which works out well.

I recently re-applied for my driving licence. I completed the form and knew it would be a long process due to my drink-driving incident. I had to pay the top price initially to even send the form off. I then got a letter and had to prove my innocence. I had to pay another £100, in cash, to get a blood test done by a DVLA approved doctor for them to decide if I were to be issued with a licence. Finally, I got the all clear and I received my driving licence. It does feel like I can't ever be forgiven for my alcoholism and I seem to constantly have to prove myself and always give more effort than the average person. In this case I do understand, it would be totally unacceptable for the DVLA to issue a new licence to a known offender. However, when I called to book the appointment, I was told to just not have a drink the night before.

If that's all it shows up, then there is a serious loophole in their process and seems more like a money-making scheme but that's not for me to comment. I hadn't had a drink for years so had nothing to hide. It was a bit soul destroying going through the how much, what made you start etc. talk yet again and I wonder if it will ever stop. It seems like at least monthly something happens that my previous problem doesn't affect. Always having to justify myself is tiring. I just want to move on with life. I accept what I did was wrong. However, I also accept that the things I did weren't me but was the ill, addicted version of me. I wasn't well and I have understanding and compassion for the old me. I used to run around like a headless chicken not knowing what I was doing, wanting to stop yet not being able to.

I've hurt a lot of people during my alcoholism. I think I've mostly apologised but never know when it stops. I could apologise daily for everything I did but I don't think it will help anyone. I just need to live life, one day at a time, drink-free. I need to be caring to myself and others now by being allowed to move on from that chapter in my life.

Wayne and I quit smoking about three years ago. We switched to vaping so aren't completely off the nicotine but we're not puffing all the additional chemicals into our bodies. So, I'm drink-free and smoke-free. I still have to fight the sugar cravings but that's probably just because I always feel the need to have some kind of vice. I only got a sweet tooth when I stopped drinking. I continued with the photo shoots and attempt at modelling for a couple of years until I couldn't continue with a full-time job. To really be successful you have to go to as many auditions as possible which I didn't find feasible whilst working full time. I'd done what I set out to do and I'd picked up a couple of little jobs, nothing big, and I was content with that. I could relax knowing that I'd tried it and it wasn't for me/I wasn't for it and that I would have no regrets in the future of not having tried. What I did learn was that glamour modelling really isn't glamorous. I'd spend hours in poses on hard floors and nearly every photo involved arching my back. I'd be freezing cold and achy when I'd finished a shoot, but it was worth it to say I'd done it.

I certainly got to know who my real friends were during the madness of alcoholism. I lost contact with most of my friends, whether that due to them being too embarrassed to be seen out with me, me isolating and not contacting anyone, or friends I had decided to not see again as our only connection was alcohol. Few remained close and stuck by me no matter what. I couldn't believe how some people used me as gossip. For example, stories got back to my mum that I had been seen staggering along the street when I hadn't even been drinking for months. It was like because some people knew my past it gave them the opportunity to have a bitch when they fancied it. I remember calling my friend once as she was going through a difficult time. I was sober and had been for months when she started ranting at me that it wasn't fair that she was ill and I was fine, she screamed that I should be the one suffering and not her. This was a huge blow to me, and it felt like she was sticking pins in a voodoo doll of me. I didn't say anything and let her finish her rant, but it left me feeling hurt and raw. It didn't matter that I had got clean, it still seemed to give some people an excuse to have a pop at me and use me as their punchbags. Another friend once called me when I was suffering a particularly bad withdrawal and I told him how Mum and Div were so worried. His response was they were probably worrying about covering the costs of my funeral, which was not what I needed to hear while I was already at my lowest. This friend I cut out of my life entirely as it was someone I had been on binges with and I didn't need people like him in my life anymore. I had to be caring to myself and removing people from my life who were dangerous was a must for me, besides I thought it was a vicious thing to say.

I'm a completely different person now. I know we all change throughout our lifetime but for me the changes have been quite drastic. I still do weird things and some of my thoughts are a bit obsessive, like writing this book. Once I started, I couldn't seem to stop. I get a great sense of achievement from finishing things. Unfortunately, that doesn't leave much time for rest but I've learnt over time I have to have me-time even if it's just sitting reading or listening to meditation music. When I was at The Centre a previous client got trained in reflexology. For a donation to The Centre (it is a charity), I was able to have a few sessions with her and really felt the benefits of feeling more grounded and less all over the place in my head. I also tried reiki and got on well with that. I am currently training to be a spiritual healer. It's the first thing that has really sat right with me and I feel like it is something I am meant to do. I'm always reading books on spiritual subjects and healing and it also helps me to heal in the process. My main aim every day is the same - to not pick up a drink.

MY 'RULES'

During my recovery, I read my fair share of self-help books. It almost became yet another type of addiction until I calmed it down and instead of trying to cram in too much knowledge, I found it best to 'do' rather than just read the books. I did learn quite a bit about myself from reading, also from generally being sober as it opened a whole new world to me. I started to know my likes and dislikes and over the time of my sobriety I think I have changed a great deal. I now try to incorporate some of the methods I've read about into everyday life. This sounds like I'm making life hard work, but I've found much more happiness by following some of my own 'rules' which I will share now in no particular order.

STAY FOCUSSED

My mind still wanders continuously, and I seem to have a million things going around in my head at any one moment. I have a habit of multi-tasking and can start something simple and mundane like cleaning and end up doing all other jobs in between, so I now just try to get the job at hand done and to the best of my ability. Staying focussed is all it takes and incorporates being mindful, and in the moment, rather than worrying about the past or future. Thoughts still go around my head but with the focus, it gives my mind a little rest. Generally, I try to stop faffing and get the job done without my head interrupting me.

IF YOU DON'T GO WITHIN
YOU GO WITHOUT

Although I like to keep myself busy and focussed, I've also learnt that no rest is no good. I always try to set some time aside for myself every day to just be peaceful and rested. This can involve reading, lying in the sun, taking a stroll outdoors or meditating. It clears my head and gives my body time to relax and unwind. I find this is a hugely important factor that I just must do. I have to shut out the outside world and go into my own bubble. This has led to me having much more awareness of myself. It's during the quiet times that I have random thoughts pop into my head that I had never given any thought to previously, it's like the quiet talks to me and gives me inspiration. I no longer have any distractions at home. I find it much more peaceful when I am at home alone to just hear the noise of the birds rather than listening to the TV or radio. It's during these times that I feel most rested and at ease.

BE CLEAN!

Obviously, during some of my darker times I struggled with hygiene and was unable to even wash. I remember clearly during one of my very ill times trying to complete the simple task of brushing my teeth. It was so much effort and drained my energy. I struggled to stand up so had to sit and even then, the movement of my hand brushing my teeth took the energy out of me, and that was with an electric toothbrush. When I finally completed it I felt like it was a real victory and something I would never take for granted again. During the same bout of illness, my skin was extra dry and flaky. I couldn't even muster the energy to put some body lotion on my legs as I was so exhausted, and I vowed that when I was better, I would always take good care of myself. Part of this rule now is that I always get myself ready first. That advice was given to me years ago by a mother of six boys. She once said, "If you don't get yourself ready for the day before doing anything else then you will never be ready". I took this advice on and always prioritise me being ready before I start anything else. I like to know I am ready for the day before I get distracted and I now take pride in my hygiene and appearance.

YOU HAVE TWO EARS AND ONE MOUTH FOR A REASON

A classic from Trevor. This is so true, and I needn't say any more on the subject as it speaks for itself.

EXERCISE

I try to exercise daily although it's not always possible. I've tried all sorts of exercising at home from my collection of DVDs and found yoga helpful. Any exercise is worthwhile. Most of us always use the excuse of being too busy but I've found some ten-minute yoga sessions that I can always manage to fit into my day, every day. It does become a bit of a chore and adds to my mental to-do list, but I believe it's very worthwhile. When I'm older I don't want to be struggling about, I've missed out on enough by struggling. I want to be as fit as I can be and the only way to achieve it is to incorporate exercise. There are many excuses I've heard as to why people can't exercise but there is always something that can suit each person, no matter how little or how much effort it takes.

MEDITATE

I never thought I would be able to meditate. I won't lie I'm not great at it, but I give it a good go. I used to turn my nose up at meditation but that was because I didn't really understand what it was all about. In nearly every self-help and spiritual book I have read they suggest incorporating meditation into your life. There must be something in it or not as many people would say the same thing. I started small with just ten minutes. I found guided ones helped at first as they give you something to focus on, rather than having your mind wander. Over time I have increased the times and started to meditate in silence which is even more difficult. This is when my mind clears, even if just for a few seconds at a time. I'm getting there, gradually. These days I try to be kind to me, and this is something that brings peace of mind and clarity.

CHANGE THINKING

We all have a habit of thinking we know best but sometimes we have to take advice from others and see it from a different perspective. I used to be so set in my ways, I still am at times, but I've learnt to be a lot more open-minded and I am open to taking new approaches in looking at issues. I've done a lot of work on myself through group therapy and it's hard. Not many people can say they work on themselves. I always try to be open to new views and outlooks and not afraid to keep working on myself. If I didn't change my thinking, then nothing would have changed. It's the thinking that changed the drinking. If you keep going about things in the same way you can't expect different outcomes.

JFDI

Stop procrastinating and just do it! There are a lot of things I want to do and like others, I used to think *I'll start tomorrow.* Nowadays when there's something I really want to do I make the first step in achieving it. I wanted to write a book and it took five years until one day I thought, *I'd only have to start it.* Without that first step, no one would get anywhere. There's no time like the present and life is a gift.

SAME TWENTY-FOUR HOURS AS EVERYONE ELSE

Back to the old don't have time subject. I get really annoyed with people that tell me that I'm lucky I have time to exercise, meditate, or go on evening courses and that they are just far too busy. They then spend five minutes telling me how they are too busy to be able to do whatever it is they want to. I always think in that five minutes they could have started whatever it is they are saying they don't have time to do! We all have the same twenty-four hours in a day. It's what you fill your time with that matters. People say they don't have time, yet you hear them chatting about a computer game or TV show they played or watched the previous night. It's how we prioritise the time that matters so I believe that you need to find the time to do whatever it is you love or want to do. That can take as little as ten minutes a day - ten minutes of focus rather than faffing.

STICK TO WHAT YOU SAY YOU WILL DO - AND DO IT

People are full of ideas of what they would like to do but never seem to get around to doing it, so it ends up just being a daydream. I've lost out on so much valuable time during my illness that I now value my time and what I do with it. If I say I will do something, then you can pretty much guarantee that I will. There's no point always telling other people you will do something then not follow through with it as over time they just won't believe you.

TREAT YOURSELF

I've been hard on my body over the years and now I think it's time to look after me with a bit of pampering. I try to book in, at least monthly, a massage or a spiritual healing session. No excuses for not having time. I believe it's extra important to unwind and relax my mind and body. I always have a clearer head and am much more present after having any kind of treatment. It's my way of treating myself and taking care of myself.

KEEP NOTES

I often read books that have something I find very inspirational in, but if you ask me the following day what it was, I often can't remember. Now I jot things down as and when I see them. Sometimes I will find a quote I like or see a plaque on a wall somewhere. I keep a small notebook in my handbag and note it down so I can look back on it. I also get to the end of books where there is the section that recommends other reads. Recently I've made a note of anything that grabs my attention, so I don't forget the next time I want to download a book. It's too easy to forget things as we all lead such hectic lives but carrying a notebook around can be helpful. One inspirational quote I read by John F. Demartini in The Breakthrough Experience, got me through to finishing this book. I don't think I would've completed it without reminding myself, *'By the mile it's a pile, by the yard it's hard, by the inch it's a cinch!'*

LEARN FROM WHAT HAS HAPPENED IN LIFE

I believe that everything happens for a reason, even the bad things. If we don't learn from it then what is the point in it ever having happened? The way I see my past now is either become a victim or learn from it and grow stronger from the experience. I don't want to become a victim.

FEAR IS THE ONLY BARRIER

Fear of anything isn't nice. I know this only too well. Sometimes we are tested and if so, we need to rise above it and face our fears head-on. It's much easier said than done but this goes back to my one small step at a time rule. I still have fear in pretty much everything I do, but if I let it build up then I'd never leave the house or do anything. I tend to compare fear with the worst things that have happened in my life which makes me think *it can't be that bad.*

GET UP IN THE MORNING

I've wasted so much time lying about in bed feeling sorry for myself or being too ill to get up. I've gone the other way now where I literally can't lay in even if I wanted to. I feel like I'm just wasting precious time. Obviously, I don't tend to do things by halves, and I have calmed the getting up at 4 a.m., even at weekends, as I'm trying to be kinder to myself. If I need sleep, then I think it's very important to get as much as my body and mind needs. If, however, I am awake early and I'm not tired then I will get up and make the most of my day. I like to find out what time someone gets up after they complain about not having time to do anything. You often find they hit the snooze button ten times then laze around in bed for ages when they get a chance. Mornings are my best time of the day. I love to get up before anyone else when the world seems quiet and still. It's in this time that I can enjoy my coffee in peace then start the things I want to do. I believe if you send the message out to the universe that you can't be bothered to face the day then I don't think you will have a very productive day. When you are excited to get up as it's a fresh new day it can bring opportunities and possibilities. I also think it starts me off on a vibe of excitement for the day, rather than the vibe of can't be arsed. In my opinion if you snooze you lose.

DON'T LET OTHERS TELL YOU THAT YOU CAN'T

I've had my fair share of people tell me that, "You can't" or, "You'll never be able to" in my life. I decided to ignore them. I think it's important to make up your own mind. I listen to others' point of view, but I don't let them dictate to me what I can or can't do. I like to have some self-belief although I've struggled with this for most of my life. I like to think I've become a little braver and more willing to try the things I want to, regardless of what other people think or say.

MAKE YOUR OWN LUCK

You have to put the effort in to get any results out. For example, over the years I've won a few prizes from online competitions I had entered. The general response I get from others is, "Why are you always so lucky? I never win anything". My response is, "How many competitions do you enter?" to which the answer is always none. How can they possibly think they will win something without entering it in the first place!? The other comment I get is, you've guessed it, "I don't have time"! This applies to everything, if I'm not there, or showing willing in the first place, then I can't feel hard done by if I don't get whatever it is I am hoping for.

ATTITUDE OF GRATITUDE

I think it's important to be grateful. Before I go to sleep, I like to think of all the things during the day that I am grateful for, so I go to sleep on positive thoughts. I am also always grateful for being able to get up in the mornings and start a new day. I was so scared at times in my past that I wouldn't wake up again that I try to find gratitude in things I previously took for granted.

DON'T BLAME EXTERNAL THINGS

Take responsibility. I've taken responsibility for myself - finally. There's no point making excuses and blaming things that have happened to me, or what isn't happening that I would like to. If I take responsibility and take action, then things become my choice. This goes back to my point about being a victim and wallowing in self-pity or making positive changes. If I really don't like something in my life then I try to change it, there's no point moaning about it. I don't like feeling trapped so if something doesn't sit right with me, I have the opportunity to change it and move on. Change can be scary, but I like to know I can change anything I do not like about myself and have the ability to change my situation if I want to.

FINAL WORD

Drinking was a tough, time-consuming career. It seemed so difficult to find the help I needed. People often ask me if I think they have a drinking problem then explain how often they drink and at what time of the day. My answer is always the same, if you think you may have a problem then it has already become a problem for you, regardless of the scale of it. You wouldn't be questioning it otherwise. If you've found yourself looking up whether you are consuming over the weekly recommended units, then you've probably already recognised you are drinking too much. There is help out there, it's just not always immediately obvious. A lot of people I know are regular AA-goers. I've been a few times, but I prefer the aftercare option I found, mainly due to the late timing of AA meetings. AA are people with one mission, the desire to stop drinking. I wholeheartedly believe and support AA although I don't regularly attend meetings. Anywhere that is based on the twelve-step program I recommend. I can't quote exactly how many people it has helped as, as the title suggests, it's anonymous. Whenever I have been to meetings, I have felt the power of the group and always felt better leaving the meeting than I did when I arrived.

There are also some not-so-good places out there that just try to look good with statistics. If you have a problem don't rule anything out and keep an open mind. If you keep trying, eventually you will find something that suits you. It's very difficult as people have such an opinion on alcoholism and addiction. If you want and need to get better then keep trying, ignoring the not so great comments you will receive from many along the way. You have the power in you to stop if you really want to, after all, look at the amount of effort it takes to maintain being an active alcoholic. Switch that determination to find something that suits you and only you. Try every option available and never give up. Eventually, you will find something that feels right, maybe you'll find it on the first attempt.

I find it amazing how so many people offer advice on alcoholism when they have no direct experience of it. Would these same people offer advice to someone with a terminal illness and start telling them what they should or shouldn't do? I think the general answer is no, however when it comes to alcoholism every Tom, Dick and Harry have some pearl of wisdom to share. This is dangerous. No one wants to be an addict. It is a life-threatening illness. People offer advice on triggers and how to not drink (after all they can normally) and they think this gives them some kind of qualification on the subject. I hear the word trigger thrown into many conversations. 'Triggers' in alcoholism, in my opinion, do not exist. An alcoholic can find every excuse under the sun as to why they need a drink so could end up with thousands of triggers. Yet that seems to be the buzz word from people who don't understand it, or in my case alcohol centres that also didn't. I believe in changing the thinking, so you never need to pick up again. I'd spent hours mentally listing what could be a trigger and I'd drive myself insane as the list could go on for eternity. I could literally find any reason for me needing a drink. My advice is if you know nothing about alcoholism or addiction point the person suffering to people who do know. They need to be safe and unfortunately, Joe Bloggs' advice on the street isn't at all helpful and could potentially be harmful. It confuses matters and the alcoholic will take on any advice if it means they can somehow justify having a drink.

People offered me all sorts of useless advice when I was in the depths of my active alcoholism. Mum was told to lock me in a room and throw away the key which was great advice had she actually wanted to kill me. My pet hate was people telling me, "I don't have to have a drink to have a good time" which I am still told now. *Does it sound like I was having a good time?* The number of times I got told to start cycling as a remedy was ridiculous. It was like riding a bike was a world-known cure for alcoholism that I'd never heard of. I understand fresh air and nature can be healing but they didn't understand I couldn't even lift my head off the pillow on some days, however the advice was always to get out cycling. I don't even own a bike!

The main thing is to find other people you can connect with who understand you - other recovering alcoholics or addicts. Find people who are already in recovery and learn from them. They will truly understand you because they have already been where you are, even if you think that's impossible. If you don't know where these people are then look up the nearest AA group. If you don't want to go anywhere local then look up the surrounding area, they are everywhere if you just look. There are also lunchtime sessions if, like me, you're an early bird and in bed early. When you go to a meeting it will free your trapped mind and put you in contact with people who understand and who have experienced it in their own unique way. They can also put you in touch with helpful centres and steer you away from any government statistic-based ones that might not be any good (maybe there are some good ones out there, but I've never been successful in finding one myself). Learn from others and never try to do it alone. I can guarantee that all of us alcoholics tried going it alone until we really hit rock bottom and there was nothing left. There are people all around that are willing to help, you just need to find them. You only need one who can steer you in the right direction and from there you will meet others. Every person in recovery you meet you will learn something from. There is power from people and you will not be judged by former addicts themselves. You may think that the shameful things you have done are unique to you, but they are not. Other people have been there, and I can guarantee they have done similar, or even worse, although you probably won't believe that until you reach out. Once you start opening up to the people in recovery you will no longer feel so alone, you will realise that there are others similar to you. When this realisation sets in you can't help but see it as an illness. If everyone has similar thoughts and feelings in active addiction then it must be a legitimate 'thing' therefore can only be described as an illness or disease, or dis-ease, as some prefer to refer to it. Once you understand it is not just you that thinks the way you do you can learn how to heal. This illness cannot be ignored. In my experience when you go it alone your head, over time, starts to convince you you're OK, leading you back to the drink or drugs or addictive behaviour. It may not be immediate, and you may not see it coming, but going it alone always leads you back down the same path, the one you were so desperate to turn your back on. When you have a serious illness, you continue to get treated even if it's for check-ups. This illness is no different, it is a life-threatening disease. You need to keep yourself in check and you do that by connecting with people who understand and who can be there to support you. When you start to receive this support and realise the power it has, you may find you'll want to provide support for others as well. After all, you will have the experience to help them. Knowledge and experience alone won't keep you safe though, so make sure you stay connected with other recovering addicts in whatever way you choose.

Get yourself the help and support you need, as soon as it starts to become an issue for you. You can heal. Have patience and faith and be willing to mix with other people who truly understand. You will no longer need to feel so lonely, don't waste precious time trying it alone. Never give up hope and stay safe.

Printed in Great Britain
by Amazon